AUTHENTICITY & ACTION

BY PEACE MITCHELL & KATY GARNER

Women Changing the World Press acknowledges the Elders and Traditional owners of country throughout Australia and their connection to lands, waters and communities. We pay our respect to Elders past and present and extend that respect to all Aboriginal and Islander peoples today. We honour more than sixty thousand years of Indigenous women's voices, stories, leadership and wisdom.

Copyright © Peace Mitchell and Katy Garner
First published in Australia in 2025
by Women Changing the World Press
an imprint of KMD Books
Waikiki, WA 6169

All rights reserved. No part of this book may be used or reproduced by any means, graphic, electronic or mechanical, including photocopying, recording, taping or by any information storage retrieval system without the written permission of the copyright owner except in the case of brief quotations embodied in critical articles and reviews.

Because of the dynamic nature of the Internet, any web addresses or links contained in this book may have changed since publication and may no longer be valid. The views expressed in this work are solely those of the author and do not necessarily reflect the views of the publisher and the publisher hereby disclaims any responsibility for them.

Edited by Tracy Regan

Typeset in Adobe Garamond Pro 12/17pt

 A catalogue record for this work is available from the National Library of Australia

National Library of Australia Catalogue-in-Publication data:
Authenticity & Action/Peace Mitchell and Katy Garner

ISBN:
978-1-7640374-2-6
(Paperback)

CONTENTS

Introduction 3

The Moment of Awakening – Abbey Dyer-Amonette 7

The Joy of Being Perfectly Imperfect – Amy Hall 19

Moonlight Companion – Anila Bukhari 35

Roadmap to Becoming an International Professional – Anna Abesadze............45

Daring to Dream to the Moon and Beyond – Astra K 59

From Exhaustion to Expansion – Christie Nicholas 69

Be Unapologetically You – Dr Chela Chomicki 83

Be a 'Yes' Person with Boundaries – Dr Danielle Camer.....................................94

Staying True to You – Emma Weaver..109

From Love, Finding Purpose, Creating Change – Hayley Boswell..................119

The Courage to See – Hayley Van Loon 133

The Heart of a Purpose-Driven Life – Karen Weaver......................................147

A Manifesto of Existence – Marisa Estela 157

Shoes You! – Nouna Chugg..169

Magic Happens – Rudi Landmann 181

Unmasking the Truth – Sara Knight...193

Authenticity Architecture – Tanya Hicks 205

From Tragedy to Purpose in Making an Impact in the World – Wendy Shew...223

Harmony by Design – Yona Signo..238

"Here's to the crazy ones. The misfits. The rebels. The troublemakers. The round pegs in the square holes. The ones who see things differently. They're not fond of rules. And they have no respect for the status quo. You can quote them, disagree with them, glorify or vilify them. About the only thing you can't do is ignore them. Because they change things. They push the human race forward. And while some may see them as the crazy ones, we see genius. Because the people who are crazy enough to think they can change the world, are the ones who do."

Steve Jobs

INTRODUCTION

Showing up as who we really are sounds so simple. But is it?

For some people it is extremely difficult and even dangerous to be authentic and express their true thoughts, beliefs and identity. This is not the world I want to live in.

My highest values are freedom and connection. For me freedom is allowing others the right to be who they are, to make their own choices, to have their own beliefs, to express their own identity.

Connection means truly seeing people for who they are and connecting on a heart to heart level.

A world where everyone is free to express who they are and allow others to be who they are is a world where everyone can be their most authentic self.

So why does parts of our world, society, culture so often want to put people in a box? Insisting that everyone should act the same, think the same and be the same as they are? I don't have the answer.

When I was younger I wanted to change my name.

Being called Peace in a world filled with Sarahs, Rachels and Katherines was overwhelming. I constantly felt uncomfortable meeting new people and worried that they would think I was strange and weird for having such a different name. I'd never met or even heard of anyone else with the same name as me. When we went to a café and they asked for a name for the coffee order I would always give someone else's. I didn't want to make them feel weird for calling out for Peace. I was worried about unconscious and conscious bias too. In my mind being called Peace immediately labelled me as a Hippie. At the worst people would assume that I was someone who chained themselves to trees or was unemployed and dirty. Even at best that they would think I was unprofessional and not to be taken seriously with a name like that.

I had gone to an all girls Catholic school for my early years and with a name that reflected one of the Christian values, Peace was acceptable there. But moving to a new town where I knew no-one and being enrolled in a co-ed State school was terrifying. Not only was I the new kid, I was also the weird kid. They called me John Lennon. I know there are worse things to be called at school, but I just felt so different from everyone else.

Your name is such a big part of who you are. In later life I've learnt to love my name. It's always memorable and even the energy of this word is something so special.

In the experiment with the energy of water I know that Peace is one of the best words, so hearing this every time someone says my name or saying it every time I introduce myself has to have a positive impact on my body at a deeper level.

But as a teenager it was just hard. Noone wants to be different in high school. Being different isn't safe and standing out for all the wrong reasons can make your life miserable.

So I began to shrink. I became smaller and smaller, quieter and quieter. Not saying anything, not wanting to stand out. I was so afraid of being seen that the day I was due to give a presentation to the class my voice completely disappeared. Vanished. Gone. I ran out of the classroom

AUTHENTICITY & ACTION

in shame.

I just wanted to fit in but the harder I tried the less I did.

I was bullied because they thought my shyness was because I thought I was better than them. Because I'd previously been to a private school they also assumed that I was rich, how wrong they were. My parents drove beat up cars and we'd had to leave the private school because we couldn't afford the school fees.

I constantly felt like an outsider and I continued to shrink, becoming smaller, quieter, more invisible and alone.

Adjusting to a new environment of any kind is always hard. In every institution there are hierarchies, systems, power structures and the ways of doing things that remain unchanged over time. A lifetime of following rules in private school helped condition me on how to follow the new rules here, even though they were different and strange.

Eventually I left the first group of friends I had clung to in my early days and found my place with a different group of friends who took me in, took the time to get to know me and accepted me for who I was. Slowly I rebuilt my confidence and became more able to be myself.

It's amazing what a difference having the right circle of people around you can make. I found myself performing as the lead in the school play, finally having a best friend, being invited to parties, getting my first part time job and starting my first business braiding hair before school each morning.

Without the support of those friends though I don't know how I would have got through it. Is authenticity conditional on how safe you feel? Does it rely on having good people around you? Do we mask because we don't feel safe to be who we really are? How much does a sense of safety contribute to our ability to be fully authentic? Does authenticity take courage? Is authenticity reliant on a sense of belonging? I don't know the answers to these questions but I do know that my journey to authenticity was better because of the people I had around me and because of their support and acceptance I was able to step into my truest version of myself.

The teenage years are hard for everyone, I believe it's a time when we all go through so much angst and questions around who we are, who we want to be and who we will become. No longer children but not yet adults, there are so many uncertainties and depending on where you go to school it can be a brutal environment for exploring your identity.

I graduated high school, a lot more confident in who I was, knowing what I wanted to do, with friends around me who would be with me, and yet I still questioned whether I should change my name when I got to university.

Those first few weeks at university were eye opening, I suddenly found that the world was made up of lots of different people. My sheltered life had led me to make so many assumptions about the world, going to Catholic school had made me think that most of the people in the world were Catholic and I soon realised that there were lots of other religions and people who followed them! Not everyone came from farms or small towns and the small mindedness I had experienced at high school was not reflected here. I found that there were all kinds of people living all kinds of lives, sharing all kinds of perspectives, with different dreams and ambitions and ways of life. It was incredible!

I realised I wasn't weird at all; in fact, I was celebrated for my uniqueness. My name was the thing that made people remember who I was. Not everyone liked me, but I realised that not everyone mattered. I found the places where I belonged, the people who loved me and the courage to embrace my own authenticity.

I hope that the stories within these pages inspire you to embrace your authenticity and take action on your wildest dreams.

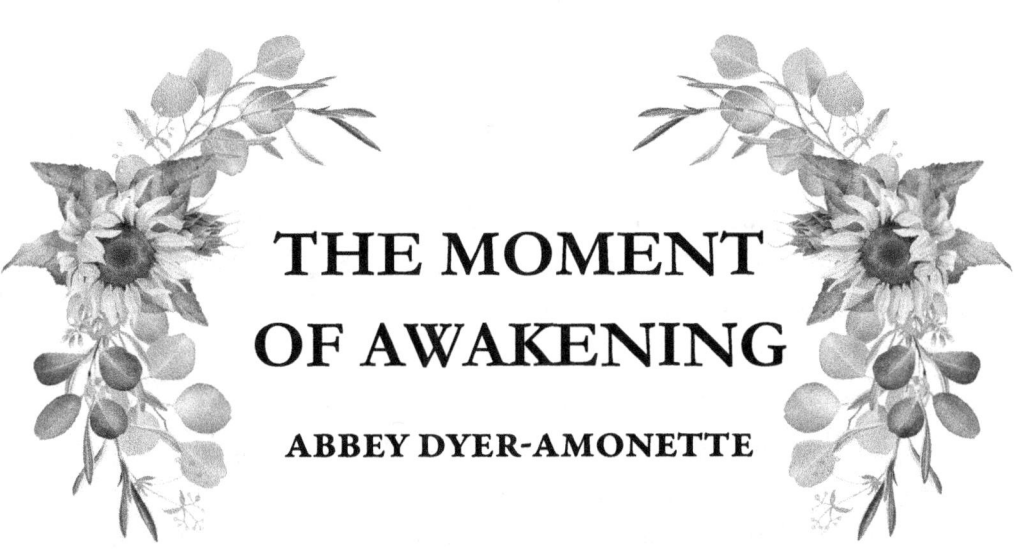

THE MOMENT OF AWAKENING

ABBEY DYER-AMONETTE

There comes a time when you realise the life you're living is no longer enough, like you've outgrown the container of who you once were and need a bigger space to breathe. That moment hit me in May of 2024, when I found myself standing on a stage in London, about to speak to a room full of incredible female entrepreneurs. On the surface, it looked like a typical speaking engagement but in my heart, it felt like a portal into a new dimension of possibility.

I'd been invited by two brilliant women I deeply admire (Christina Rowe and Hayley Hall) seven-figure entrepreneurs, to share my insights on artificial intelligence (AI) - truth be told, I didn't feel nervous about speaking. I've always been that curious blend of introvert who lights up when sharing knowledge with an entire audience. The stage somehow feels safer. Go figure.

I felt an electric tingle in the air. The kind you get when you know something important is about to happen. I began speaking about AI and how it can revolutionise your business. The more I talked, the more I realised I was touching on something far deeper than just technology.

As I wrapped up my talk, I felt my heart pounding, not from fear, but from exhilaration. It was like my soul was whispering, *This is what you're meant to do. This is who you're meant to be.* And that whisper felt both terrifying and exciting. I walked off stage with possibility, and for the rest of my time in London, I moved through each day with an extra bounce in my step. When I hopped on the plane home, I thought, *Wow, life might never be the same.*

And it wasn't.

The moment I returned to my home office and opened my corporate email, all that glittering excitement faded. My London bubble popped. The tasks, the meetings, the corporate structures, felt small compared to the big vision dancing in my heart. After 25 years in corporate leadership, where I'd coached, mentored and guided thousands of people, I suddenly felt claustrophobic. My gut was screaming, *You've outgrown this. There's more for you out there.*

What did that mean? I wasn't entirely sure. But I knew I had to find out.

"Your next leadership role isn't a dream, it's a decision. Set a goal, make the plan and claim your seat at the table."

THE EARLY YEARS: HUSTLING FOR A BETTER LIFE

To understand why that moment in London rocked me so much, you must know where I started, why the idea of leaving something "secure" behind felt both liberating and terrifying.

Let's rewind to a younger version of me, juggling three jobs. At one point, I was a grocery cashier, a bow-maker (yes, custom bows!), and a medical receptionist. Somehow, amid all that, I was also putting myself through college. When people ask what I majored in, I sometimes say "survival." It's only half a joke.

Looking back, I understand how much my undiagnosed ADHD played a role in my struggles. Textbooks felt like mountains of words that wouldn't stick. Lectures drifted past like the haze of daydreams. And on top of that, I was raised in a conservative community I never quite fit into. I rebelled ... a lot, numbing the discomfort with alcohol. But behind all that rebellion, behind the late nights and the questionable decisions, was a longing: *I want to do something meaningful in this world. I want to serve others and live a life of purpose.*

Eventually, I gathered my nerve and made my great escape to Washington State. To my younger mind, it was the farthest place from home. I arrived wide-eyed and ready for a new chapter, immersing myself in non-traditional spirituality, crystals, anything that felt expansive. I devoured books on meditation, hoping to uncover a hidden key to the life I wanted.

Then came network marketing. At first, it felt like destiny, a chance to blend personal growth and financial freedom. But sometimes, what seems like a shortcut turns out to be a long detour. A nutrition company promised riches, and I went all-in. Three years later, I emerged divorced, $50,000 in debt, and feeling like I'd been dropped on my head.

Still, I kept hustling. I worked in healthcare and juggled side gigs, photography, nail polish, essential oils; anything that helped me feel less stuck in the matrix. In 2011, my partner and I started an artisan leather goods company. I look back on that time with a weird mix of pride and exhaustion. I was running a thousand miles an hour, but the question kept nagging me: *Why am I doing all of this?*

LESSONS FROM LOSS: DEBT, DIVORCE AND DETERMINATION

That question became unavoidable, staring at my pile of bills and heartbreak. I remember stacks of credit card statements and thinking, *how in the world did I get here?* But there's a special kind of determination that rises when you feel like you've hit bottom. You realise that if you survived this, maybe there's not much you can't do. Deep down, I was still that woman who craved genuine impact and freedom to live life on my terms.

In 2015, after about 17 years in various corporate leadership roles, I could see the glass ceiling. We were subtly (and not so subtly) told to play by the rules if we wanted to be accepted. It was exhausting. I gleaned so much experience, but kept wondering, *Is there a better way?* The answer was *yes*, and I hoped I could be part of creating that better way for other women.

That's around the time I first dreamed about helping women step into their power. I wanted to show them how to break free and build lives that felt good, rather than just looked good on paper. The idea buzzed in my mind. But before I could bring it to life, we got a phone call that changed everything.

THE ADOPTION THAT CHANGED MY WORLD

Stepping back a bit, for four and a half years, my spouse and I tried to have a baby. Month after month, test after test, disappointment after disappointment. Months turned into years. We sought fertility specialists and I endured endless tests, shots. My body felt part science experiment, part pin cushion. My emotions were like a broken roller coaster, stuck in a loop of hope and despair.

When we finally got pregnant with twins, we were over the moon. We told a small circle of people. Sadly, not long afterward, we lost them. I can't fully describe that heartbreak, and maybe I don't need to. If you've been there, you know. If you haven't, just imagine having your deepest wish dangled in front of you, only to have it snatched away without warning.

I felt broken. I didn't know if I'd ever truly be "okay" again. As the physical and emotional pain sank in, one thing became clear, my body and mind had reached their limit. We had always planned for adoption, so we pivoted and opened ourselves to the path that was calling us all along.

AUTHENTICITY & ACTION

Once we chose adoption, we discovered it has its own brand of waiting and uncertainty. There's paperwork (so much paperwork!), background checks, home studies, and a lot of hoping someone will see something special in your story. We worked with an agency and after 18 months of no guarantees, we got "the call."

Of course, it happened in the middle of my busiest 1/1 corporate healthcare season. I was on a conference call, my spouse opened my office door, rocked her arms like she was rocking a baby and pointed down at the floor, whispering "BABY, TODAY". I told my team I needed to wrap up the conference call and practically flew out of my chair.

We found out our baby boy had arrived sooner than anyone expected. There wasn't going to be a three-or-four-month lead-in with the birth mother. It was a *drop-everything-right-now* scenario. I'm a planner by nature, so I immediately launched into action mode: *We need a car seat! And diapers, and clothes, and a stroller, and... everything else a newborn needs!*

About thirty minutes later, we were on the road, to meet our son. We chose a name, secured an attorney and called our families during the drive. Underneath the nerves was the deepest sense of *rightness* I've ever known. It was like my heart whispered, *Of course this is how it happens. This is how you finally become a mom.*

"Success doesn't happen by accident. It's created by intentional action, an unshakable effort, and a belief in what's possible."

Those first days of motherhood were a blur of joy, exhaustion and tears. I was still healing from the loss of the twins, so I felt like a walking contradiction; broken and whole at the same time.

By the time my son was one, we knew something was different. My son was later diagnosed with autism and ADHD, which we lovingly call our "special brains." For six years, my world revolved around therapies, specialists and making sure he had every opportunity to thrive. And guess what? He's doing amazingly well.

During those years, I pressed "pause" on my coaching dreams, but I never forgot them. In 2021, when my son had gained so much independence and confidence, I felt that tug again; *It's your turn. Go do the thing you've always said you would do.*

THE DECISION TO STEP FULLY INTO MY PURPOSE

That tug got a megaphone when I traveled to London in May 2024. Something about being in that vibrant city, speaking on stage about AI, ignited a fire I couldn't ignore. It was the same nudge I'd felt years before, but this time it roared, *Now. Not tomorrow. Now.*

I came home, sat at my corporate desk … and felt nothing. The job that once felt so exciting now felt suffocating. I realised that for 25 years, I had done incredible work. I made a difference. But it was time for a different kind of difference. I set a date, a year out, to leave my corporate role. It felt both thrilling and heartbreaking because the people I worked with had become my second family. I cared about them. I cared about the projects and the mission.

I remember a meeting not long after I returned from London. My boss was giving me my performance appraisal and I broke down in tears. Not the quiet, polite tears you can dab away with a tissue, but the ugly cry that comes from deep in your gut. I think he knew it was the beginning of the end of my corporate chapter.

Then, in a cosmic twist, I went on a family vacation and got COVID. Great timing, right? We were at Martha's Vineyard, and instead of strolling the beaches with extended family, my little family was isolated. Funny enough, that forced stillness was exactly what I needed. For a week, I had no choice but to rest, reflect and revisit that internal voice saying, *It's time. You can't keep waiting.*

Somewhere between coughing fits and cold rags, I reached a place of

AUTHENTICITY & ACTION

deep peace. I realised I was trying to hold onto two realities at once, my corporate identity and my soul's bigger calling. Letting go wasn't easy, but it was necessary.

Once I made the decision, I felt like a giant weight had been lifted. Of course, that weight didn't vanish overnight. For a few months after I left corporate, I found myself mentally wondering if my old team was okay. *Should I have stayed longer?* But the clearer my vision became, the more those doubts faded.

I remember sitting down one evening and writing what would become my mission statement:

I help women live a life full of aligned purpose, authenticity, freedom and joy.

As soon as those words spilled onto the page, I knew it wasn't just some cute mantra, it was a call to action. If I was going to help women live that way, I had to live it first. *Talk about accountability!*

And that's what brought me here, sharing these words, hoping they'll land in the heart of another woman who's on the fence, wondering if she can really break free from what she's always done to step into who she's meant to be. The answer, in case you're wondering, is yes. Yes, you can.

Because here's what I've learned:

You can be scared and ready at the same time.

You can feel broken from past losses and still walk bravely into a new future.

You can care deeply about the people in your current environment but still move on to something more aligned.

And when you step onto that stage - literally or metaphorically - to share your gifts, something magical happens; you come alive in a way you never have before.

And that, my friend, is why it's called **The Courage to Be Seen**. Standing in your truth, owning your experiences (the good, the messy, the painful), and daring to say, "This is who I am and what I'm here to do." That's not just some marketing tagline, it's a revolution in how we as women show up in this world.

But courage alone isn't enough. You also need **The Strength to Step Forward**, that determination to move, act and create change in your life. Because knowing you're called to something bigger is one thing - actually doing it, is another. The world needs your light, your gifts, your story and your fire … right now, not next year.

So here I am, forging a path that blends AI with heart-centred business coaching. Leverage cutting-edge tools to serve more people, make a greater impact and still stay aligned with our souls. We can build businesses that let us have coffee dates with our best friends (or ourselves!), volunteer at our kids' schools, and take spontaneous afternoon naps if we darn well please. Freedom isn't a luxury, it's a calling.

The truth is, the world is waiting for you. And it's waiting for me, and for every other woman who has that inkling in her gut saying, *I was made for more.*

I promise you, if you listen to that voice, you'll discover a life that isn't just successful on paper, but deeply meaningful in your heart. That, for me, is the definition of joy. And that is why I do what I do.

I'll leave you with this question: *What is one step you can take today to honour the bigger life you know you're meant for?* It doesn't matter how small it seems. A single step forward can ignite a chain reaction of miracles.

Because **The Courage to Be Seen** is about embracing your truth, scars and all.

And **The Strength to Step Forward** is about choosing, every single day, to follow that truth wherever it leads.

The world is waiting for you. Are you ready?

ABBEY DYER-AMONETTE

Abbey Dyer-Amonette is a trailblazing AI expert, business coach, and the visionary CEO and Founder of Lead with Positivity. Under this platform, she has launched innovative initiatives such as Global Girl Technology and Tennessee Girl Technology, creating opportunities for women to thrive in technology and leadership. Abbey is dedicated to helping women step into their full potential by cultivating confidence, emotional intelligence, and collaboration—all while balancing professional success with personal fulfillment.

With over 25 years of leadership experience, including a highly successful tenure as a corporate executive with a Fortune 500 company, Abbey has firsthand knowledge of the challenges women face in leadership roles. Drawing from her extensive expertise, she developed her transformative signature program, Positive Feminine Leadership™, which empowers women to embrace their authentic leadership style, master emotional intelligence, and lead with strength and compassion. Through this program, Abbey has helped countless women achieve long-lasting success in both their careers and personal lives.

In October 2024, Abbey's innovative and transformative contributions to artificial intelligence and leadership were recognized on a global stage when she received the First Place Award for Women in Tech, Science & Engineering from the Women Changing the World organization. This prestigious honor underscores her commitment to empowering women leaders and driving innovation in traditionally male-dominated fields.

Abbey takes a holistic approach to her work, combining strategic leadership principles with personal development techniques. As a Certified Life Coach, Neurolinguistic Programming (NLP) Practitioner, and Reiki Practitioner, she integrates these practices to help her clients unlock professional success while achieving personal well-being. This unique blend of expertise enables Abbey to guide her clients on a journey of growth, resilience, and empowerment.

Whether you are a seasoned executive looking to amplify your leadership impact or an entrepreneur ready to scale your business, Abbey is here to guide you every step of the way. Her work is dedicated to equipping women with the tools, strategies, and support they need to create meaningful, lasting success while embracing their unique strengths and authentic selves.

THE JOY OF BEING PERFECTLY IMPERFECT

AMY HALL

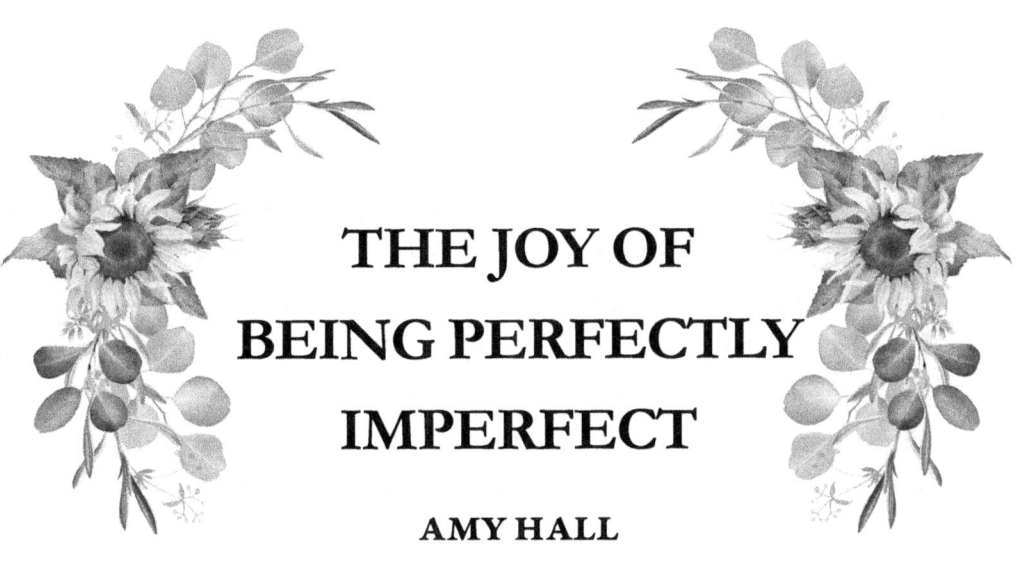

F or Berenice Murphy - A lighthouse and the greatest model of authentic living I have ever known. Being your daughter is a journey and a privilege.

I have always loved trees. They can be pruned, shaped and nurtured into the most magnificent forms, yet they still grow with a mind of their own; reaching toward the sun, following their own innate design. Trees can be trained to grow in a particular way, but in the end, they will root in the soil, grow up or out and develop the way the environment and their DNA governs them.

Similarly, people have an inherent power to create the intricate and ever-evolving picture of who we are. They make choices that shape their relationships and the world around them. The philosopher, Joseph Campbell said, *The privilege of a lifetime is being who you are*. However, being who you are requires more than privilege - it demands self-awareness, courage and unconditional self-love.

When we allow external forces - society's expectations, fear of rejection, or unkind voices - to shape our choices, we risk living a life misaligned with our true selves. We become actors, performing for the approval of an audience. Without their applause, we convince ourselves we have no value.

It wasn't until my late 30s that I realised I'd been chasing approval for too long. It was time to hear my own voice, trust myself and embrace who I truly am. By leaning into self-awareness, courage, vulnerability, self-compassion, boundaries, connection and living my values, I let go of the fear that had kept me suspended for so long.

Authenticity is the result of infinite growth, shaped by recurring acts of self-discovery and resilience and the willingness to show up, be seen and exist just as you are.

Today, at 40, I feel a deep sense of peace, strength and freedom. This chapter reflects my journey to authenticity and the affirmations that guide me. I hope it inspires you to embrace your own perfectly imperfect self.

SELF-AWARENESS: THE SEED OF AUTHENTICITY

Self-awareness is the foundation upon which authenticity is built. It's fuelled by knowing and trusting yourself.

Growing up, I often felt emotionally unsafe and misunderstood. As an undiagnosed Autistic/ ADHD girl, the world around me didn't make sense and I struggled to find my place in it. My thoughts and feelings were often dismissed as dramatic or exasperating. Even my memories were reframed or invalidated, leaving me to doubt my reality. I learned that to be accepted, I needed to *correct* myself to fit others' expectations.

In my late 30s, a mentor planted a life-changing seed: *"What if you aren't a problem to fix? What if you are enough, exactly as you are?"* These words forced me to confront my deepest fears about myself. Could I trust that my feelings and thoughts were valid? Could I like myself without needing anyone else's approval?

I really wanted to like myself. I rarely looked in the mirror; at the

AUTHENTICITY & ACTION

time I was 140kgs and had no idea what food really tasted like, I just ate to fill up a hole in me that kept getting bigger. I mostly wore black or dark clothes to shrink myself as much as I could. I knew I wanted *to feel* differently.

The answers didn't come overnight. Through a process of self-discovery and acceptance, I learned to prioritise emotional safety, stepping toward people and experiences that nurtured me and away from those that drained me. I chose to trust myself. It wasn't easy. Experimentation and loneliness were part of the journey and I lost quite a few relationships along the way. I also lost 60kgs. I now look in the mirror and smile … and I rarely wear black. Ultimately, each choice to honour my needs reinforced the belief that *how I feel and who I am is enough.*

Dolly Parton says, *Find out who you are and do it on purpose.* For me, self-awareness is a lifelong practice in trust, choice and reflection, as well as the foundation that allows my sense of authenticity to grow.

VULNERABILITY: THE BIRTHPLACE OF CONNECTION

Brené Brown describes vulnerability as emotional exposure, risk and uncertainty. I think it's the birthplace of connection.

I've always been described as an oversharer. For some, my openness was 'too much,' but I've never shied away from sharing my mistakes, failures and truths. Being vulnerable and transparent enables a deep connection with others and invites them to be vulnerable themselves.

But being this way isn't always easy. Some people have retreated from my life, uncomfortable with my openness. These moments are deeply painful, as I experience rejection sensitivity like others might experience a bad sunburn. Even small dismissals can feel disproportionately intense. Being vulnerable is very personal. It requires courage, and for some people, it triggers feelings they are not ready to recognise in themselves. To protect themselves, their rection is to recoil or retreat. I now respect their boundary, rather than internalising it as a rejection.

Vulnerability requires embracing perpetual uncertainty, but it also creates the most profound connection both with yourself and your relationships. It challenges me to stretch, adapt and embrace both the beauty and the pain of being fully seen, which is a true gift to the world.

COURAGE: PERSEVERING THROUGH THE BREAKS

Maya Angelou said, *Courage is the most important of all the virtues because without courage, you can't practice any other virtue consistently.*

For me, courage was choosing to stay alive, even when every thought in my mind conspired for me to end my life.

My story is one of surviving deep depression, unmanaged impulse control, untreated ADHD, and chronic anxiety. For years, *shame* was the lead actress in my narrative, joined by her co-star, *dread*, together, both convincing me the world would be better off without me in it. Fear played a powerful supporting role as a blinding spotlight and a persistent shadow, keeping me trapped in survival mode.

Fear is like a cactus; thorny and imposing. Yet, I discovered these thorns guarded a reservoir of insight and strength. Marianne Williamson reminds us that, *Our deepest fear is not that we are inadequate, but that we are powerful beyond measure.*

My fear wasn't just about my perceived shortcomings, it was the terror of stepping into my own light, of embracing the power to be unapologetically myself.

Fear loses its power when you lean into it with curiosity rather than resistance. When I step toward what fear tells me to avoid, I find courage quietly waiting to guide me forward. It's uncomfortable, sometimes excruciating, but it's inherently brave.

Courage has taught me that my light isn't just mine, it's a gift to the world. When I embrace it, I give others permission to do the same.

AUTHENTICITY & ACTION

Courage isn't about perfection, it's about persistence; choosing to move forward, even when the path is uncomfortable or unknown.

SELF-COMPASSION: EMBRACING IMPERFECTION

Self-compassion is about treating yourself with kindness, especially in moments of failure or pain.

I used to apologise for breathing - or speaking - such was the weight of my self-loathing. Now, I only apologise when I owe it, as a bridge to resolution or to make amends. I no longer feel guilt for making mistakes; the most universal of human experiences. I now appreciate them as opportunities for learning. This mindset shift profoundly changed my life for the better.

Self-compassion is the most challenging value I have cultivated. It is a daily habit of humility; of repeatedly cracking open my heart after every error/disappointment/frustration or upending life experience, and filling it with gratitude and grace; not criticism, doubt or blame. I credit this wisdom to my husband, who has always seen me as perfectly imperfect, even when I couldn't see it myself. His unconditional support has made practicing self-compassion a much easier choice.

At times, I fall back into old patterns of feeling like a burden, especially when I am unwell. When I need extra help in hospital, recovering from illness, or when anxiety is shouting loudly at me and I am working hard to reclaim my composure, I catch myself apologising to my husband for taking up space or feeling like a burden. But rather than saying 'Sorry', which is about guilt and self-loathing, I say 'Thankyou' which reflects my gratitude for his gift of holding space for me.

When I hear the inner voices reflecting shame, dread or fear, I acknowledge it, find a mirror, look at myself and smile, even when I am crying or raging. I repeat this affirmation until the voice is replaced with compassion.

This is temporary. Today was tough. Feel this, remember this, let this teach you what you need to know - Trust the universe- she knows what she's doing. You are enough, just as you are. I know who you are, and I love you.

Self-compassion is embracing imperfection and trusting in my ability to navigate life's challenges, just as I am, whatever may come.

SETTING BOUNDARIES: AN INNATE ACT OF SELF-LOVE

As a young woman, my boundaries were shaped by a desperate need to fit in. I overextended myself, agreeing to things that made me uncomfortable or drained me, all to avoid risking rejection. I was like a house with no walls, exposed to the elements, unprotected and vulnerable to being shaped by others' expectations.

As I grew into self-awareness, boundaries became a definition of self-respect.

'No' is a complete sentence, requiring no justification or apology.

Saying 'no' when the choice didn't align with my values was necessary to create space for what truly mattered. I walked away from relationships, jobs, family members, leaning into the fear of being hated and alone, believing this preferable to the reality I had settled for.

By recognising your limits and expectations, boundaries are implemented by good communication, compassion and the acceptance that these will not be received well by some people. In fact, it may trigger them and lead you to be criticised or attacked.

When this happened to me, boundaries helped me recognise this criticism as misalignments without needing to internalise them. When people don't respect my boundaries, they reveal their truth. I've learned to listen, trust their actions and graciously wish them well on a journey that no longer intersects with mine.

Boundaries give me clarity to grow in alignment with my values and the freedom to connect with others, as I've strengthened the edges that

AUTHENTICITY & ACTION

hold our relationships together.

THE KEY TO MEANINGFUL CONNECTION IS RECIPROCITY

In my work, children who are non-speaking seek connection through different behaviours, and some of these are unsafe, maladaptive and often misunderstood. My job is to help others see what these children need to achieve this connection safely. I am privileged to have learned from these young people; joining them in their world on their terms and experiencing the utter magic when they look and smile at you; the recognition that they feel seen and accepted, just as they are.

Connection occurs in fleeting moments, often in conversations or simply holding space for vulnerability. When people feel safe, they can reveal their whole soul, even when you don't know their name. I look for these opportunities every day. They fuel me.

Relationships, like a shared meal, should be reciprocal, where people contribute and receive. This is the nourishment that results from beautiful moments of shared truth and connection through vulnerability. The singer, Jessie J remarked, *"Why would you stay at a table, and contribute a plate of food, while never being fed?"* This resonates deeply with me when I think about connection.

If you're constantly giving without being nourished in return, you're sitting at a table of depletion, not connection. Choosing to leave a few of these those tables has been one of the greatest decisions I've made.

My husband offers me a transformative, profound connection. His quiet, unwavering belief in me has mirrored the parts of myself I have struggled to love. His acceptance taught me the power of being surrounded by people who celebrate, rather than merely tolerate me. He has also taught me the power of silence and holding space, and how just being present in all my forms, moods and mindsets, strengthened and emboldened me in ways I never thought possible.

Connection is a ripple effect of authenticity - when you show up as yourself, you invite others to do the same.

LIVING YOUR VALUES

Learning about and living my values has meant staying true to my beliefs, even when it required challenging the systems around me.

I have always struggled anywhere where those in authority prioritised conformity over creativity and compliance over compassion. Values that mattered to me - empathy, innovation, experimentation, relationship - were often at odds with the priorities of these systems. Instead of fostering collaboration and growth, these systems demanded the status quo; the ease of 'the way it's done' and essentially, leaving limited room for individuality.

In my work, I realised that compromising my integrity was no longer sustainable. Aligning my work with my values was essential, not just for my well-being, but for creating the kind of meaningful impact I wanted to make in the world. Creating my business aligned to these values was a powerful proclamation of stepping into authentic living.

My business was born from a drive to offer a service that was human-centered, flexible and in a partnership with our clients. It also serves as a vehicle to challenge policies and practices that I vehemently disagree with. Currently, this includes the practice of physically restraining or secluding children in schools when their behaviour is perceived as unsafe. These practices are wrong. At best they are unhelpful, at worst, traumatic and potentially catastrophic. I use my voice as loudly as I can to agitate for change, to speak against these practices and offer alternatives that are evidenced-based and non-aversive. I speak up for the children who are locked in cages and cannot speak for themselves.

Banksia reflects my commitment to learning from my clients,

understanding them to empower a greater quality of life. It's about providing a map for connection, safety and growth while modelling how to self-advocate so the world will believe in their inherent value and worth.

THE JOY OF KNOWING YOU ARE ENOUGH

Oprah summarised her life in one sentence - *I teach people to lead their best lives by leading my own.* In my own way, I hope to do the same.

My journey in authenticity hasn't been a straight line. Each experience, whether painful or triumphant, has contributed to the design of my life, unfolding as an evolving process.

I want to be remembered as someone who stood up for others, showed kindness and made people feel seen and loved, just as they are. I hope people remember my optimism, courage and resilience, as well as my sheer determination and tenacity to dive into the unknown, fear be damned. I started my business with little more than my passion, wits and a belief that I could be the captain of my own ship. And I have found more joy than I ever thought possible. Every risk was worth it.

I haven't quite worked out the sentence that sums up my life and purpose. But perhaps this chapter has encouraged you to reflect and cultivate your own.

AMY HALL

Amy Hall: Advocate, Educator, and Leader in Behaviour Support

Amy Hall is a dedicated teacher, youth mental health advocate, and Child & Adolescent Behaviour Support practitioner with over 20 years of experience supporting vulnerable populations. She holds multiple university degrees in Education, Leadership, Youth Work, and Mental Health Advocacy and is planning to commence a PhD candidature in 2026.

Her professional journey is deeply personal, rooted in her own experiences as an Autistic woman with ADHD and a disability, navigating the challenges of self-discovery, resilience, and living authentically. Amy has faced and overcome significant barriers. These experiences have shaped her belief that disability is not a limitation but an opportunity to demonstrate resilience and leadership.

As a trusted advocate, Amy specialises in promoting social inclusion and supporting families across Australia who live with complex disabilities. Her expertise lies in helping children and young people who display unsafe behaviours due to unmet or misunderstood needs. Amy's mission is to foster understanding about her clients—who they are, why they behave in different ways, and how their communities can enhance their quality of life. By building skills and creating proactive support systems,

AMY HALL

Amy helps reduce the need for restrictive practices, a critical focus in Australia's disability sector.

Amy is an internationally recognised leader, earning multiple awards for her contributions to disability advocacy and business leadership. As a sought-after speaker, she shares her lived experience of disability and connect with her audience, sharing insights on resilience, inclusion, and the power of embracing one's true self. She also speaks about her successful entrepreneurship journey inspiring others to embrace resilience and innovation.

Beyond her direct work with families, Amy collaborates with government organisations to develop best-practice approaches for supporting children with disabilities in hospitals, schools, and workplaces. She is a passionate advocate for sector capacity building and serves as the clinical supervisor to a wide group of Behaviour Practitioners nationally. Recently, she launched a groundbreaking national training program for Behaviour Practitioners, aligned with Australia's National Disability Insurance Scheme (NDIS) behaviour support capability framework—one of the first of its kind in the country.

Amy's philosophy of the "two-degree shift" guides her work: the belief that even small changes in a person's trajectory can create profound, lasting impacts on their future. This philosophy mirrors her own journey, where seemingly small moments of self-awareness and courage led to transformative growth and a deeper sense of purpose.

Amy's work exemplifies her unwavering commitment to improving lives, building understanding, and inspiring others to recognise the power of inclusion and compassion. She is a leader who stands for change, empowering individuals and communities to embrace the potential of every person, regardless of their circumstances.

Amy's life and work are testaments to the power of authenticity, connection, and courage.

AUTHENTICITY & ACTION

Her chapter offers readers a deeply personal glimpse into her journey, alongside practical lessons for embracing their own perfectly imperfect selves.

Website- Amy Hall
Website: www.banksiasupport.com.au
Linked In: (3) Amy Hall | LinkedIn

MOONLIGHT COMPANION

ANILA BUKHARI

The moon has been my faithful companion since childhood. Even after fifteen years, its soft glow brings back vivid memories of my journey, like scenes from a film playing on an endless reel. I remember sitting on the lawn, tears streaming down my face, mourning the loss of butterflies. Their vibrant wings, once symbols of fleeting beauty, now lay still and silent.

'Why, God? Why did they have to die?' I cried out in anguish, my heart weighed down with grief. The sight of their lifeless bodies, a wound that lingered long after my tears had dried. As I gently touched their delicate wings, another wave of sorrow washed over me.

This moment sparked something profound within me. Every morning, I began searching for dead butterflies, carefully burying them in tiny graves. I couldn't bear the thought of anyone stepping on these fragile creatures without a second thought. Over time, I came to realise that my empathy stretched beyond the butterflies to the injustices I witnessed around me.

In my community, girls and women bore the crushing weight of a patriarchal society. Their freedoms were stripped away; they were silenced and treated as subordinates. My aunt's life left a deep mark on my heart.

She was a prisoner in her own home, robbed of even the simplest of joys.

At the age of seven, I could not fully grasp why so many women around me seemed resigned to hopelessness. Some couldn't visit their parents without permission, let alone dream of independence. I once asked my aunt, 'Why are you so sad? You're not allowed to shop, work or even visit your family without your husband's approval. Isn't this cruel?'

Her tearful response planted a seed of resolve within me. Even as a child, I felt a deep urge to challenge this cruelty - not just for myself, but for the women around me who had no voice.

By the time I turned ten, I had begun observing the world with fresh eyes, searching for answers to the injustices that troubled me. Chasing fireflies became my favorite escape, their glowing light a fleeting moment of joy in an often harsh reality. Each time I caught one, I felt as though I had grasped a bit of magic, a reminder that beauty and hope could still be found.

I also found solace in my grandmother's stories, which were rich with tales of courageous women who defied the odds. Sitting by her side, I felt connected to their strength and resilience. Her stories reminded me that I was not alone in my struggles and they kindled a growing belief that I, too, could make a difference.

The moon, once a silent observer of my grief, became a symbol of my journey toward self-discovery and empowerment. Its gentle light felt like a guide, urging me forward even in moments of doubt.

As I reflect on my journey, I see it as a delicate yet determined unfolding of petals, shaped by the moon, the butterflies, and the women who inspired me. Though my path is far from complete, I am certain the moon's light will continue to guide me toward a future filled with justice, hope and strength.

A JOURNEY OF LOVE, LOSS AND LITERATURE

My mind takes me back to one of the most painful moments I've ever

AUTHENTICITY & ACTION

experienced. It was the day my uncle arrived at our door and said, 'Anila, your granny passed away.' Those words pierced my heart like a dagger, leaving me shattered and adrift.

I remember the overwhelming sense of suffocation, as though the world had stopped. My beloved grandmother - my companion, my guiding light - was gone. The thought of never seeing her radiant smile again, never hearing her comforting voice or feeling her warm embrace, was unbearable.

I vividly recall visiting her grave, tears streaming down my face as I touched the cold stone. 'Granny, why did you leave me?' I cried, my voice breaking under the weight of my grief. 'Can't you see I need you? I feel so alone without you.' But the only response was silence; a hollow void that seemed to echo my despair.

The night before she passed away remains etched in my memory. I had slept beside her, holding her frail hand and telling her how much I loved her. She had smiled weakly, her eyes brimming with love and I had asked her why she wanted to leave us, why she couldn't stay forever. She kissed my forehead gently and whispered, 'Stay strong, Anila. I will always be with you.'

Those words became my anchor, a mantra that reminded me of the resilience she instilled in me. My granny was more than a grandmother, she was my best friend, my confidante, my soulmate. Her heart overflowed with kindness. She always put others before herself, giving selflessly without expecting anything in return.

I treasure the memories of our time together; the laughter we shared, the bedtime stories she told and the unconditional love she gave. She had a way of making me feel seen and heard, validating my emotions and encouraging me to chase my dreams.

One of my dearest memories is of the day she bought me a doll and a hair wig I had longed for. She never once questioned my choices or dismissed my desires. Instead, she supported me with a love that made me feel like the most important person in the world.

When she passed away, it felt as though a part of me had died with her. But as I reflect on her life and our time together, I realise she left me with an invaluable gift; a love of writing.

I began writing at the age of ten, pouring my emotions into the pages of my journal. No one in my family had ever written a book, but I was determined to break that mold. I wrote poems, stories and articles, sending them to journals and magazines, hoping someone would recognise my voice.

The journey was anything but easy. Rejection letters piled up, doubts crept in and there were moments when giving up seemed tempting. But my granny's words echoed in my mind, urging me to persevere, to keep writing and to never lose sight of my dreams.

After six long years of persistence and heartbreak, my efforts bore fruit. My stories began to be published in magazines and digests; people started noticing my work. The same digest team that had once overlooked me now invited me to write for them. It was a surreal and deeply rewarding moment; one I will cherish forever.

Looking back, I realised that my granny's passing was not just a profound loss but also a lesson in resilience. It taught me to treasure the time we had, to find strength in adversity and to channel my grief into something meaningful. Her unwavering belief in me inspired me to keep writing, to stay true to myself and to never abandon my dreams.

Though she is no longer physically with me, her legacy lives on in my words. I will continue to write, to tell the stories that need to be told and to inspire others to do the same. And whenever I feel lost or alone, I will close my eyes, remember her loving words, and find the strength to carry on.

FROM STRUGGLE TO SUCCESS

I am overwhelmed with gratitude and humility. My path as a writer has been anything but smooth - filled with struggles, setbacks and moments

AUTHENTICITY & ACTION

of doubt. Yet, it was determination, faith and a commitment to kindness that ultimately paved the way for my success.

I vividly remember the countless nights I spent writing by candlelight, as power outages were a constant reality in my area. But I refused to let those challenges hinder me. I poured my heart and soul into my work, driven by an unwavering belief in my dreams. My mother was my pillar of strength throughout this journey, always encouraging me and lifting me up when I felt low. Each time I posted a manuscript to a digest office, I would ask her to bless it with a prayer. Her love and blessings became my guiding light, giving me the courage to keep going.

There were times when the darkness, both literal and figurative, felt all-encompassing. In those moments of despair, I cried out to God, seeking guidance and strength. It was during these heartfelt prayers that I discovered the transformative power of faith and perseverance.

Looking back, I see that my journey was not solely about achieving success but about growing into a better version of myself. I learned that to truly succeed, one must first strive to be a good person; a devoted daughter, a supportive sibling and a compassionate member of society. Kindness, humility and empathy are the foundations of true achievement.

Today, I am proud to call myself the author of thirteen best-selling books. I share my knowledge by conducting free workshops on candle-making and other crafts. I have been honored with numerous international awards. Yet, my greatest achievement is finding inner peace and living a life of purpose.

This journey has taught me that success is not merely about fame or material wealth but about living with intention, making a difference and staying true to oneself. The struggles I faced, though difficult, shaped me into the person I am today. For that, I am deeply grateful.

ANILA BUKHARI

Anila Bukhari is a renowned champion of girls' education, a passionate children's rights advocate, and an award-winning humanitarian. Born in Pakistan, Anila has dedicated her life to empowering marginalized communities, particularly rural areas, underprivileged women, and victims of child marriage.

As a prolific author, Anila has penned 12 international bestselling books that inspire and educate readers about the importance of girls' education. Her work has taken her to over 50 countries, where she has raised her voice against child marriage and advocated for girls' education.

Anila is the founder of the Butterfly Wings Global Teachers Club, which provides education to rural girls. She has also established a safe haven for survivors of rape, depressed, poor, and needy girls, including child widows. Anila offers free education to over 1,000 rural girls, teaching them valuable skills such as candle-making and providing workshops on financial independence through her project, Girls Shine.

Anila's commitment to education extends to creating free little libraries in underserved communities. She has established 15 libraries in 15 countries, including Georgia, Dubai, Turkey, Azerbaijan, Poland, the UK, USA, Nepal, and Pakistan.

AUTHENTICITY & ACTION

Through her tireless efforts, Anila has become a beacon of hope for girls and women worldwide. Her selfless dedication to girls' education has

[12/19, 10:46 AM] Meta AI: Here's a rewritten biography in the third person, within the 500-word limit:

Anila Bukhari is a renowned champion of girls' education, a passionate children's rights advocate, and an award-winning humanitarian. Born in Pakistan, Anila has dedicated her life to empowering marginalized communities, particularly rural areas, underprivileged women, and victims of child marriage.

As a prolific author, Anila has penned 12 international bestselling books that inspire and educate readers about the importance of girls' education. Her work has taken her to over 50 countries, where she has raised her voice against child marriage and advocated for girls' education.

Anila is the founder of the Butterfly Wings Global Teachers Club, which provides education to rural girls. She has also established a safe haven for survivors of rape, depressed, poor, and needy girls, including child widows. Anila offers free education to over 1,000 rural girls, teaching them valuable skills such as candle-making and providing workshops on financial independence through her project, Girls Shine.

Anila's commitment to education extends to creating free little libraries in underserved communities. She has established 15 libraries in 15 countries, including Georgia, Dubai, Turkey, Azerbaijan, Poland, the UK, USA, Nepal, and Pakistan.

Through her tireless efforts, Anila has become a beacon of hope for girls and women worldwide. Her selfless dedication to girls' education has earned her numerous international awards and recognition. Anila's story serves as a testament to the transformative power of education and the impact one person can have on the world.

ROADMAP TO BECOMING AN INTERNATIONAL PROFESSIONAL

FROM ASPIRATION TO ACTION

ANNA ABESADZE

Have you ever had an inner hunger to make a broader impact? Those who have, will affirm that it's not just a passing thought - it's a persistent, almost unexplainable pull to the soul. It's the quiet yet powerful call to contribute to something far larger than oneself; something that transcends personal achievement. This drive isn't about fame but about leaving a legacy of meaningful change, staying true to yourself and finding the rare inner peace that whispers: 'This is why you're here.'

And yet, this calling comes with an urgency so intense, it can evoke a fear deeper than failure; the anxiety of leaving this world without fulfilling your mission. It's a reminder that life is finite, and the time to create impact is now.

Choosing to operate on an international scale, isn't always about the inability to make a difference locally. A small town or country can be the perfect ground for meaningful change - if circumstances allow. But often, political, societal or systemic constraints can suppress your ability to act, forcing you to work within rules that limit your vision. The international stage, however, offers a different kind of promise; the freedom to explore opportunities unbound by local restrictions. It's a space where creativity thrives and bold steps lead to meaningful change that touches lives, far and wide.

Moreover, gaining international experience allows you to bring valuable insights back to your community and country, empowering you to become a true agent of change. While working in the US, I came across an opportunity to fund two bright, underprivileged students from my hometown, providing them with scholarships for a year; an opportunity I might not have had if I'd been in Georgia at the time. Similarly, I found time to mentor students virtually, offering guidance and sharing my experiences. In today's connected world, if you're willing, you can be an agent of change, no matter where you are.

Take Oprah Winfrey, for example. Born in the quiet, rural heart of Mississippi, she faced systemic racism and personal struggles that could have defined her. But through resilience and a deep sense of purpose, she rose to become a global media icon. Picture her journey, a young girl with big dreams, her voice once unheard, now echoing across the world. Oprah didn't just break barriers, she redefined them. She embraced the global stage, using the platform to spark conversations, uplift communities and inspire change on a scale few could imagine. Her story reminds us that when you carry the lessons of the world back home, you don't just create change - you become the change.

So here's the question: How do you turn the dream of an international career into reality, taking that first step toward a journey that inspires and empowers others?

DEFINING A CLEAR AND AUTHENTIC VISION

If we don't know where we're going, how can we expect to end up in the right place? Without a clear vision, life can carry us along like a river, and before we know it, we may be in a place that doesn't feel right—somewhere we're unhappy or don't belong.

AUTHENTICITY & ACTION

To find our way, we must first get real with ourselves and figure out our WHY. Why do we want what we want? What truly matters to us? Once we understand that, the HOW - the steps we need to take – will start to make sense. It's so important to stay true to yourself and figure out what you really want, not what looks good because someone else has it or seems happy with it. Their path isn't yours. Their joy isn't yours. You deserve to live a life that feels right for you - a life built on your own dreams, not someone else's story.

I've always known I wanted to work with international organisations; places where my efforts could drive real change. Growing up in a small town with limited opportunities, I experienced firsthand how their projects transformed lives, including mine. As a beneficiary, I found hope, discovered new possibilities and saw the power of even the smallest support to ignite potential. That experience shaped me, turning my work into more than a job - it was a way to give back and inspire others to see beyond their circumstances. It's what drives me every day; the chance to be part of something bigger and to be the change I once needed.

Once you have a clear and authentic vision, everything changes. It becomes the North Star that guides you, no matter how long or challenging the journey ahead may seem. With that clarity, you can break the seemingly impossible into small, attainable goals - a path that brings the big dream closer, one step at a time. When your vision aligns with who you are, it fuels you like nothing else. It silences doubt, quiets comparison and awakens an unshakable determination to honour the dreams only you can bring to life.

The greatest gift you can give yourself is a life filled with meaning and purpose; a life that feels truly your own. As life comes to an end, so many people carry a heartbreaking regret - that they didn't have the courage to follow the path their heart truly longed for. They let life's circumstances, fears and expectations hold them back, and they never fully lived the life they were meant to live.

Don't let that be your story. You have the power, right now, to choose differently, to step into a life that resonates deeply with who you are, even if it feels uncertain or difficult. Because in the end, what will matter most isn't how perfectly you lived, but how authentically you did. Be brave. Create a life that you can look back on one day and say, I lived with purpose, I lived with meaning, and I truly lived.

BUILDING GLOBAL COMPETENCE

Isn't it amazing to wake up each day with a clear purpose, knowing exactly where you're headed? That goal at the finish line sparks motivation within, guiding each step with intention, helping you to focus on what truly matters, instead of drifting aimlessly.

Having a clear vision gave me the focus I needed to take intentional steps toward becoming an international professional. It shaped how I approached every decision, allowing me deliberate about the opportunities I embraced and those I let go. I set a ten-year timeline to build global competence, but the question loomed; where should I begin, and how can I be sure I'm on the right path?

For me, the journey started by looking up to the professionals I admired; people working in international organisations doing the kind of work I dreamed of. I studied their paths and mapped out my own: earn my degrees, learn a global language, gain international experience, and build necessary skills and networks.

It wasn't a quick sprint - it was a marathon that tested my patience and resilience. Besides, the journey required constant reflection and adjustment. The world evolves and so must we. Yet, the core elements of my plan remained unchanged; acquiring the knowledge, developing the skills and building the networks essential to reaching my destination. With every step, that vision became not just a goal, but a guiding light

AUTHENTICITY & ACTION

- one that kept me grounded, driven and ready to adapt without ever losing sight of where I was headed.

For me, that vision translated into pursuing international experiences and an MA that would equip me for the global stage. Besides the industry-specific expertise, it meant cultivating multicultural intelligence, mastering the English language and refining project management and communication skills, all while building a network that transcended borders. Despite financial hurdles that made studying in the US and Europe seem unattainable, I refused to let them define my limits. Instead, I pursued opportunities through competitive programs and was honoured to become both a US Department of State Scholar for an exchange program in the United States, and a European Commission Scholar for my master's degree in Estonia.

During my undergraduate years, I dedicated every holiday to participating in international projects in Bulgaria and Turkey. These opportunities allowed me to immerse myself in diverse cultures and language, strengthen my adaptability in multicultural work environments and refine my ability to build meaningful relationships across borders. Along the way, I was fortunate to meet many kind and inspiring individuals who generously mentored me, offering invaluable advice that often saved me years of trial and error. Their wisdom not only guided me but also transformed my perspective, revealing opportunities I hadn't even imagined. These experiences enriched my cultural intelligence, sharpened my professional skills and naturally connected me with extraordinary individuals. The friendships and partnerships I formed during those years have since grown into lifelong bonds, enriching my personal and professional journey in ways I could never have dreamed.

Of course, this kind of global exploration comes with its own bittersweet reality. As the writer Miriam Adeney beautifully expresses:

"You will never be completely at home again because part of your heart always will be elsewhere. That is the price you pay for the richness of loving and knowing people in more than one place."

Indeed, the world has become my home, and the connections I've made across its many corners are treasures I hold close. Each experience, each person, has shaped the vision that continues to guide me forward - one step closer to becoming the best and authentic version of myself.

THE KEY INGREDIENT TO REACHING THE FINISH LINE

Have you ever stopped to wonder why life's most successful people aren't always those with red diplomas, honour rolls or perfect grades? Why is it that straight A's in school don't automatically translate to victories in the real world? Could it be that the secret to true success lies in something far deeper than academic accolades? Unfortunately, the brightest report cards can, but don't always, predict the brightest futures.

For me, nothing has been more essential to success than grit; that unique blend of passion and perseverance that fuels the pursuit of goals, as defined by Harvard Business Review. It's about staying committed to long-term aspirations, even when the road gets steep and filled with obstacles.

One of the most transformative moments of my life was realising that my dream of studying in the US could truly become a reality through a scholarship program. The journey, however, was anything but easy. The first time I applied, I didn't even make it past the first round of the three-stage competition. But instead of letting it stop me, I made a promise to myself: I would give it my all. For an entire year, even during the summer, I devoted myself to relentless preparation. Every single day, I practiced, studied and refined my skills. When I reapplied the following year, my hard work paid off, and I made it through all three rounds, becoming a reserve candidate. Though I didn't secure the scholarship then, I turned the experience into a driving force. I took a hard look at my weaknesses,

AUTHENTICITY & ACTION

addressed them with unshakable determination and vowed to leave no room for doubt. By the time my final year of eligibility arrived, I was ready. After years of dedication and growth, I achieved what once seemed impossible - I won the scholarship.

That victory was just the start of something bigger. It opened the door to another journey filled with hard work, small wins and steady progress, leading to another incredible milestone - a scholarship from the European Commission to pursue my master's degree in Europe. From there, I set my sights even higher, creating a five-year plan to build the skills and experience I needed to work as an international professional in a global organisation.

As you can see, grit means staying committed - not just for a day, a week, or a few months, but for years - no matter how long it takes. This journey taught me an invaluable lesson; success doesn't happen overnight. It's built through persistence, resilience and the courage to keep going, no matter how many times you fall. As Robert Collier said, 'Success is the sum of small efforts, repeated day in and day out.' So, wherever you are on your journey, remember this; keep going. Your perseverance will turn dreams into reality.

Here's the real question: Can you develop grit if you feel you lack it? The good news is, you absolutely can. It's all about practicing discipline and building daily habits that, when done consistently, will lead to your success.[1]

When motivation wanes, reconnect with your vision - the deeper WHY behind your goals. Having a clear, authentic reason ignites a natural enthusiasm that propels you forward. That's why defining your purpose is so important - it becomes your compass when the path gets tough.

And yes, as cliché as it may sound, persistence truly matters. Consider Thomas Edison, who patented an astonishing 1,093 inventions, yet only

---

1   James Clear, 'Grit: A Complete Guide on Being Mentally Tough', *James Clear* (website), https://jamesclear.com/grit, accessed 11 December 2024.

four are widely recognised. 2 He viewed setbacks not as failures, but as steps toward success. As Edison famously said, "I have not failed. I've just found 10,000 ways that won't work."

Every misstep is simply an opportunity in disguise. With grit, discipline, and a steadfast commitment to your vision, your potential is limitless.

CONCLUSION

In the end, the journey to becoming an international professional is about more than the milestones you reach or the titles you earn, it's about the transformation you undergo along the way. It's about embracing a vision larger than yourself, stepping into uncertainty with courage and allowing each experience to shape the person you are becoming.

The hard work and determination have truly paid off! I'm now working with an international organisation that's been around since the 1950s and operates in over 100 countries. On top of that, I've landed my dream role at the University, where, along with an advising role, I get to lecture and share my corporate experience - something I've always wanted to do. It's been so worth it, but I also know this is just the beginning. Learning never stops. It's not only key to moving forward but also to holding your ground in such a competitive and ever-changing world.

As you navigate this path, remember; your origins don't define your destiny. What matters is the direction you choose to take. So take that first step boldly and let your vision guide you toward a life of purpose, connection and impact. The world is waiting - go make your mark.

BIBLIOGRAPHY

- James Clear, 'Grit: A Complete Guide on Being Mentally Tough',

---

2	Thomas Edison National Historical Park, 'Edison's Patents', *Thomas Edison*, https://www.thomasedison.org/edison-patents, accessed 11 December 2024.

AUTHENTICITY & ACTION

James Clear (website), https://jamesclear.com/grit, accessed 11 December 2024.
- Thomas Edison National Historical Park, 'Edison's Patents', *Thomas Edison*, https://www.thomasedison.org/edison-patents, accessed 11 December 2024.

ANNA ABESADZE

Anna is an Adviser to the Rector and an Invited Lecturer at Grigol Robakidze University and serves as the Global Governance Coordinator at World Vision International. A former U.S. Department of State scholar though Future Leaders Exchange Program, Anna spent an exchange year in Texas and completed her MA at Tallinn University in Estonia as an Erasmus Mundus scholar.

Anna's career has spanned continents, enriching her with diverse perspectives from Europe, Asia, and North America. After gaining invaluable international experience, she returned to her home country, Georgia, to give back and drive change through the transformative power of education.

Her dedication to making an impact has earned Anna numerous accolades, including the Presidential Volunteerism Award from the White House, recognition as a GESS Award Finalist for "Outstanding Contributions in Education", and the title of Woman Changemaker of the Year by the GISR Foundation. She is also a recipient of the "Leader of the Year" award at the MENA Woman Changing the World Awards and co-author of the New York-published book *Women Living Fearlessly*.

Anna's unwavering commitment as a global professional to driving both national and international impact highlights her passion for creating meaningful change, one initiative at a time.

DARING TO DREAM

TO THE MOON AND BEYOND

ASTRA K

Let me take you on a journey. A story about a little girl with big dreams who stared at the Moon through her first telescope and felt the pull of the cosmos change her life forever. It's a story about fighting to belong in places where you feel invisible, about learning to turn doubts into fuel and about discovering the power of resilience. As I share my highs, lows and the lessons I've learned, I hope this chapter reminds you that no dream is too big when you dare to believe in yourself and the future you can create.

'Begüm! Begüm!' my parents shouted, their voices echoing through the quiet night. But I did not hear them at first. My eyes were fixed on the Moon through the lens of my very first telescope. I was just twelve years old when I stared at the Moon closely for the first time, and its mysteries pulled me in like nothing ever had. Every night since I had brought my telescope home, I would wait impatiently for the sun to set, eager to escape into the cosmos. I would drag a chair onto our apartment balcony, carefully set up the telescope and watch the universe unveil itself as the stars glimmered to life. That night, as I turned my gaze away from the Moon and toward my parents standing in the doorway, I saw their smiles - not of frustration, but of pride. 'You have been up there for hours,' they teased, 'but we are glad to see you finding your path.' I did not know it at the time, but their words became a quiet reassurance, an anchor for the challenges I would face in the years ahead.

From that day on, my aspiration for the cosmos has never ceased. As I gazed at the Moon through my telescope, a thought crystallised in my young mind: *I want to become an astrophysicist.* The very word felt foreign in Türkiye, where most people had never heard of such a career. It sounded impossibly ambitious in a society where practical careers were valued above all else, especially for women. When I tried to explain my dreams, I was often met with confusion or skepticism. 'How will you survive in a field dominated by men?' they would ask, their brows furrowed in concern. To them, the idea of a girl working in the space industry seemed absurd, almost laughable. I learned to smile politely and nod, but deep down, their doubts did not discourage me, they fueled me.

Still, the journey was not easy. I remember one day at school, sitting alone during lunch as a group of friends laughed behind my back. 'Why don't you stop pretending to be so smart and just have fun like the rest of us?' one of them sneered. Their words stung, but I refused to let them shake me. It was not just their words that cut deep - it was their actions. My classmates would take my belongings, snatch my space books and notebooks and hide them, taunting me for my love of academics and the stars.

My classmates struggled to comprehend my fascination with the universe, questioning why I chose to discuss celestial phenomena rather than partake in their violence, including games or whispers of gossip. I was often alone, absorbed in a book, as the laughter and chatter of others filled the air. Despite this isolation, my devotion to the stars remained steadfast, strengthening my determination to one day find a community that would share my dreams and appreciate the profound beauty of the night sky.

AUTHENTICITY & ACTION

At that time, many people assumed that pursuing a career in space meant leaving Türkiye, but I did not want to abandon my country to follow my dreams. Leaving felt like an easy way out and I wanted to create a path for others to follow here first. I resolved to stay and pave my way as an engineer, knowing it would be my steppingstone toward studying astrophysics abroad. I envisioned a future where I could establish companies that would inspire others, particularly girls from my hometown, to dream boldly.

As I shifted my focus to mechanical engineering, however, I found myself stepping into yet another male-dominated world. I was often one of only a few girls in my classes. It did not matter how hard I tried, I felt invisible, overshadowed by the belief that engineering was not meant for women like me. During group projects, my ideas were often overlooked and I would watch in silence as the boys took credit for the work I had contributed to. There are moments when I wanted to walk away, to give up and pursue something easier. But then I would think about that telescope, the Moon, and the fire it lit inside me. My goal transcended becoming an astrophysicist or engineer; it was to create a world where young girls who dream of the Moon no longer face barriers to belonging.

Maturing and learning to disregard what others think you are worthy of does not happen overnight. Throughout the years, being discriminated against, constantly having to prove my worth, began to take its toll. The challenges I faced did not just leave me questioning societal norms, they made me question myself. As a young girl, I often struggled with my mental health, grappling with feelings of isolation and inadequacy. These struggles followed me as I grew older, intensified by the pressures of excelling in male-dominated fields.

At first, I saw my mental health as a weakness, something to overcome. Then I realised it was a critical piece of human experience that could not be ignored. This realisation took on a new meaning when

ASTRA K

I began researching the mental health challenges faced by astronauts. Spending long periods in isolated, confined and extreme environments has profound psychological effects, with astronauts reporting symptoms of depression that jeopardise mission safety (Slack et al. 2016). This highlighted for me that space exploration is not just about engineering spacecraft or studying celestial bodies, it is fundamentally about understanding humanity.

How do we take care of our minds and emotions while pursuing the unknown? This question deepened my appreciation for interdisciplinary research; the blending of science, psychology, engineering and art to solve complex problems. It wasn't enough to build rockets, we needed to build systems that supported human well-being. As I delved deeper into mental health in space, I realised that the future of exploration relies on collaboration across disciplines. Engineers, scientists, psychologists, artists, they must come together to address challenges that no single field can solve alone. Space exploration is not just about reaching the stars but about bringing humanity with us. Together, we can create a future where no dream is too big and no one is left behind.

I carry the weight of the little girl I once was, staring through her telescope, longing for something more. She felt the sting of being overlooked, the ache of isolation and the pressure of proving herself in a world that doubted her. Yet, she also felt the warmth of her parents' pride, the fire of her own determination and the unyielding pull of the cosmos. I stand here today not just for her but for every other girl staring at the night sky, wondering if her dreams are too big. They are not.

I have seen the barriers women face in STEM (Science, Technology, Engineering and Math), and I have felt the sting of being underestimated. I have also witnessed the transformative power of community, the strength that comes from collaboration and the limitless potential of dreaming without fear. My own life is proof that when we combine discipline, empower others and stay true to our passions, we can achieve what once seemed impossible. Together, we can push boundaries and redefine what's possible. Together, we can inspire the next generation of dreamers to reach for the stars.

Let me leave you with this: Somewhere out there, a little girl is staring at the sky, her heart racing with the possibilities of what lies beyond. She does not know it yet but her dreams are valid, her voice matters and her future is brighter than the stars she admires. I see her now and I know that she will rise - not just because she dares to dream - but because we, together, dared to believe in her.

WORKS CITED

- Slack, Kelly J., et al. *Evidence Report: Risk of Adverse Cognitive or Behavioral Conditions and*
- *Psychiatric Disorders.* National Aeronautics and Space Administration, 2016, https://humanresearchroadmap.nasa.gov/evidence/reports/BMed.pdf.

ASTRA K

If there is one word that captures my essence, it is visionary: someone who indulges in seemingly impractical dreams. For me, the most meaningful progress begins with daring to imagine what others deem impossible. As an astrophysics enthusiast, mechanical engineering student, and physics minor, I dedicate my life to breaking boundaries and inspiring others to embrace their potential.

My story began at the age of 12, staring at the Moon through my first telescope. That moment ignited a lifelong fascination with the cosmos and planted the dream of becoming an astrophysicist. Despite being accepted into the highly esteemed astrophysics program at UC Berkeley, I made the bold decision to remain in Türkiye. My choice was driven by a commitment to contribute to my country's scientific landscape and inspire the next generation of dreamers.

In addition to my academic pursuits, I am conducting pioneering research on astronaut mental health under the supervision of Prof. Lucienne Thys-Şenocak with Institutional Review Board (IRB) approval. My research explores how isolated, confined, and extreme environments impact psychological well-being and investigates the role of art in addressing these challenges. This interdisciplinary approach has deepened my understanding of how hum anity can not only survive but thrive in the

ASTRA K

most demanding conditions, both in space and on Earth.

As an entrepreneur, I founded ShareDream and AstraDine to channel my passion for innovation and collaboration. ShareDream, currently in the design phase, is a global platform created to connect dreamers with shared goals, fostering meaningful connections and empowering individuals to turn their aspirations into reality.

AstraDine, a space food research company, was inspired by my exploration of the link between nutrition and mental health. Recognizing that proper nutrition is essential for emotional resilience and cognitive performance, AstraDine develops nutritionally optimized solutions for extreme environments. By combining science, sustainability, and creativity, AstraDine is redefining the future of space dining while addressing humanity's evolving needs.

I am also the co-organizer of GALActic, an annual space-themed gala that celebrates innovation and fosters interdisciplinary collaboration across industries such as fashion, engineering, and gastronomy. GALActic will unite thought leaders and visionaries to reimagine the possibilities of the future.

Also, as a crew member of Mars on Earth Project's (MoEP) Life Support Systems team and the coordinator of Koç University for MoEP, I work on designing sustainable and habitable environments for Türkiye's first analog station and future space exploration.

Fueled by resilience and a firm belief in the transformative power of collaboration, I aim to inspire others to dream beyond limits, contribute meaningfully to humanity's collective journey, and believe in the boundless potential of imagination.

FROM BREAKDOWN TO BREAKTHROUGH

AND THE NEXT BEST STEP

CHRISTIE NICHOLAS

21 September – personal diary entry

'I'm amazed at how truly sad I am. I feel hopeless, horrible, revolting, ugly, broken, disgusting. I do not know what reserves I have left but I don't believe it's much.

I'm saddened because I believe that if and when you work hard and put in the effort, the rewards come but now I know it is not true.

I am embarrassed to talk to anyone.'

It's been 14 years since I started my business.

I never thought I'd run a business. I'd been raised by small business owners as parents who drilled into us from young, *'Whatever you do in life, never run a business.'* It was advice coming from the heart, to protect and guide us towards a better future. Working seven days a week came with so much personal and physical sacrifice. They didn't want their children to stress in the same way they had.

Initially, I listened to them and chose another direction. Their values were ingrained in me.

I had a good corporate marketing job but, one day, I read an article about, 'Forward Thinking Regret' that posed the question:

'In 10 years from now, what would you regret not having a go with today?'

I knew instinctively it was having the guts to start a business, against all expectations of me and the path I 'should' take. I wanted to prove to myself that I could do this.

The exercise itself gave me a taste of visualising something unfathomable and giving myself permission to dream. So now what?

I started a business.

For the next fourteen years, I worked through enough limiting beliefs to secure evidence I could run a successful business and prove to myself, that I am, indeed, a capable business owner.

But was I happy?

For me 'happy' is living in alignment with what makes you feel good and investing your energy on what lights you up and others around you, for the majority of your time.

There was a flaw with what I was doing. You see, in my corporate career I used to run events as part of my role and swore to myself at the time, *'Whatever you do with yourself in the future, never run events. Too hard.'* Ironically, my business was built around events.

They were high risk and came with massive pressure on many fronts that, as a result, seeped into other areas of life. I would wake up, go to sleep and have the shadow of the next event on my mind. I cared so much. I had high expectations of them, and of me. If they failed ... I failed.

I did the *hard* for a living now. It was rewarding in the beginning because who I was becoming in the process, outweighed the how. I learnt everything about business through these events. Sales, marketing, cashflow, relationships, operations, risk assessment, leadership and everything in between. It was my playing field.

Cracks started to show on a personal level when I finally realised

AUTHENTICITY & ACTION

that my whole identity was wrapped up in what I was doing for a living. I had proven to myself, through events, that I could run a business. But I was perplexed because if I moved on from what I was doing, was I a failure?

I questioned whether I could make an impact beyond my current abilities. I knew deep within that the only way to find out was to close a chapter and open another. I kept the feelings down and instead, 'soldiered' on, and diversified the business enough to open my imagination.

A new forward-thinking regret revealed itself. I again asked myself: *What will I regret in ten years time, not having a go with today?* I stood in the kitchen and told my husband, 'If I'm going to continue this business, I'm going to shape it in a way that lights me up entirely. I want a business that has a global footprint! I want to be on stage sharing stories, lessons and to help others transform in positive ways. This is where I need to go,' I enthusiastically exclaimed.

The desire was ignited. Once again, this was unfathomable to me and others, given I have only ever travelled once overseas on my own, currently in lockdown, with no end in sight.

Unfortunately, like anyone running a business at the time, what happened over the next few years was the most challenging of times economically, and yet we … I … survived. These big dreams I held were put on hold as the business was in and out of survival mode. It was harder than ever to get a break and see predictable, sustained growth, even though I was more skilled and experienced than ever. There was so much pressure.

Concurrently, niggling thoughts and voices from within unsettled me.

Go outside and feel the sun, the voices said. I'd hear this every day. I never listened.

After a particular meeting with a client, I'd noticed I felt triggered, like I'd had a dopamine hit that 'sprung' me into action. I realised then, how dependent I had become on external situations to motivate me. Unsurprising given external situations had controlled so much of our lives for years. Only now, I was aware it was happening.

I was working so hard, checking boxes, and doing all the 'right things' expected of me to rebuild the business beyond the long-term economic effects of the pandemic. And yet, the harder I worked, the less results I saw. I was numb.

Years later, I read a definition for this: *Because we're disconnected from our Future Selves, we opt for near immediate goals or dopamine hits. This short-term seeking ends up costing our Future Selves big*, by renowned psychologist Dr Benjamin Hardy, in his book, *Be your Future Self Now*.

I didn't know what I liked anymore.

I didn't know what anything tasted like.

I was walking around like a shell of myself. I was normal on the outside, disintegrating within.

I woke up and went to bed with the weight of a bowling ball on my head.

That is the only way I could describe it.

I felt unusual sensations. Depression perhaps.

Yes, I was aware, grateful and functioning. Guilty even, because I had so much goodness in my life too. *There's always someone worse off*, I thought.

Did that mean that this is how life was to be? I felt as if I was sitting on a yacht in the middle of the sea, with not even a breeze to move me along.

The year continued like this, with me clinging onto hope that something miraculous would happen before the end of the year to prove it was all worth it.

AUTHENTICITY & ACTION

18th December – personal diary entry
'I am so lost. I try so hard and I wonder: What I am doing? Why do I do what I do?
What is my alternative? I am craving proof of why I should bother…
I know it's always darkest before the dawn.'
Instead, I had a mental breakdown.

One day just before Christmas, I fell into a crying heap, feeling like the biggest failure. I had to accept that I was deeply unhappy, all my efforts throughout the entire year were fruitless. I did not have the stamina to repeat another year in the same way. And ultimately, I had no idea what I could do to turn my life and feelings around, so I could find my purpose and live life in alignment with what lights me up.

I turned to a friend too, to share what I was feeling. I told her I was grieving myself! I felt like I was having an outer-body experience. I didn't recognise myself, my feelings. Even my voice was starting to feel foreign to me. I was scared.

Ever so pragmatic, she insisted I go to the doctors for tests and a checkup. This sounded so simple, but in my bleak bubble, I had never thought of doing this.

This is what friends are for. To listen to you, without judgement and to guide you. I immediately booked an appointment. Hope kicked in.

Days later, during a meditation session, these words came through me.

'Letting go of something you truly desire is the greatest form of courage.
You release it to the Universe. You acknowledge it, you value it.
But if it is not in your life without efforting, it is not for your highest good, right now.
You have other lessons to learn first.
When you have learned these lessons bigger and better rewards will come.

You are allowed to be sad. To grieve what you thought was for you.
Then when the grieving is done, the healing begins.
You will continue to be shown this lesson until you have learnt it.
Continue to practice having an intention with feeling, then honestly let is go to the Universe.
It doesn't mean you don't want it.
It means that you welcome it easily and effortlessly.
The Universe has better plans for you.
Trust that the Universe can see things you can't.'

I felt a shift stirring within me. Things would never be the same again.

These words are now printed and framed, a constant reminder each day when I wake up.

Shortly after, I got my medical results. I was largely anemic and my central nervous system was beyond fragile. The doctor explained that this can trigger depressive feelings, tiredness, and for me, constant feelings of desolation. I audited my healthy habits and immediately put measures in place to rebuild myself to an optimum state.

This was step 1 and included getting support from other wellness experts, skilled with what I needed. It made sense to seek help for my health, just as I seek help for business.

29th December – Personal diary entry

'What if you did an experiment for next year and simply enjoyed joy?

Imagine it's the end of the year and you spent the year enjoying joy. What did it look like?'

This visualisation itself was rewarding. I saw myself and how I would show up in each day across all areas of life. And so, I made a decision. This next year for me, the focus was to enjoy joy and not take things so seriously. As I enjoy joy, I would:

Enjoy nourishing foods

Enjoy nature

AUTHENTICITY & ACTION

Enjoy sunshine

Enjoy stillness

Enjoy good company

Enjoy positive outings

Enjoy releasing pressure

Enjoy creative pursuits

Enjoy the work I do

Enjoy the clarity

Enjoy awareness

Enjoy the business

Enjoy thoughts, people and experiences that bring joy, so I can be better placed to support others

Joy enriches all areas of my life.

Joy. Joy. Joy. Joy. Joy. Joy. Joy. Joy. Joy. Joy. Joy. Joy. Joy. Joy. Joy.

The best thing was the simplicity of it all. More than twelve months on, I am still living in the moment of seeking the joy in *everything*. Even though situations didn't change, how I was looking at every situation did. I view work, business and life with a new lens. I simply focus on the next round of joy available to me, all around me, in abundance.

I made *joy and expansion* my focus for that year and on. I reviewed and redefined my values and what I want in accordance to this, rather than what I think I should want as a mother, daughter, business owner, friend, etc. Just me.

I am a more active participant in my life. I have a higher vision for myself and listen to who I am being called to become next. As a result, I set myself more unfathomable, unproven and enthralling goals to aspire for in business and life. Who do I get to become, just by having a go?

A few of the shifts I committed to, beyond being bolder in business, was with my health. I made small, consistent improvements including sleeping more, eating better and getting expert help.

I invested in relationships that truly mattered to me and nurtured them continuously. The more time I spent with the people I was aligned with, the more fulfilled I was.

And personal development was now an even greater part of my life because I loved it. I was curious about it, and it excited me. This meant I immersed myself in learning, reading and identifying new ways to expand for myself and others.

Through the falling, failing and now the focus on Joy, I chose to honour my SELF. And in doing so - my big hairy audacious why – is to live an adventurous life and show my girls how living in alignment with your purpose is normal, encouraged and possible.

If you have ever experienced a time in your life where you were:

Empty, Depleted, Numb, Insecure, Guilty, Overwhelmed, Uninspired, Sad, Directionless,

… know that this pain is your sign that there is *better* available to you.

If you are ready to explore the next phase of your life from this period, here are six practical lessons and strategies to open the doors to a more positive future:

AUTHENTICITY & ACTION

Lesson	Next best step
Others' values are not your own. You can define, refine and change your values to suit you.	Annually review your values and periodically check in to iterate any habits to reflect your values.
Reflect on your future. What will you regret not having a go with today?	Do what you will regret not doing, because it will set you free and you will grow as a person. If need be, start slow. And investigate the resistance you feel because it is usually a limiting belief no longer serving you. The sooner you address it, the faster you live by what you want for yourself.
You are not what you do.	Pursue the effect you want to have on the world and others because it will fuel you. Whether it is through paid work or not.
It is darkest before the dawn.	The past is the past. What can you change about the future and the direction you are heading?
Your health is invaluable. This includes mental, physical, spiritual and emotional.	Do your own health audit and take small steps to improve, get support where you can and enjoy the benefits it brings you and others around you.
Enjoy joy in the little and big things.	Give yourself permission to enjoy joy and feel good.

Life will be different when you dare to dream. Dare to feel. Dare to try. Even though it may be uncomfortable most days. In doing so, you live consciously. It doesn't mean you won't run off course. That's life – it is a constant course correction, and it will be easier to steer the ship again in the next best direction.

At the moment, metaphorically, I'm still on that yacht, but this time, I see exciting destinations ahead. I have more ability to operate the yacht and now there is wind in the sails and momentum around me, as I hope – for you too.

What will your life look life when you too choose joy?

CHRISTIE NICHOLAS

My epiphany came via a press release. It was 2005 and as a global-toy company's marketing manager, I was signing off on their press release an agency had prepared. Except my heart sank. Even though I wasn't a Mum then—I now have two teenage daughters—I knew the brand messaging didn't connect to the audience buying the product.

Mums.

The world's most powerful consumer, Mums control around $23 trillion in global annual spending. But brands and agencies failed to understand Mums don't want jargon, they want honesty. That was the moment I decided Mums deserved better and brands could be better.

In 2009 I opened Australia's first growth marketing agency, Mumpower, exclusively representing brands Mums buy. Now, as Australia's most experienced authority in the Mum-marketing space, I'm a speaker, author, podcast host and entrepreneur with global impact and money-can't-buy insights and experience.

My mission is to lead a movement that educates, empowers and enables Mum-centric businesses to go further—and to involve Mums in the brand dialogue.

That's my professional 'why'. My personal one? I'm responsible for

CHRISTIE NICHOLAS

showing my daughters what a big, happy, adventurous life looks like. I take happiness and living in alignment with personal values very seriously!

Mumpower has partnered with 500+ brands across all categories including iconic brands Coles, Kmart, Spotlight and Dyson and introduced the socialmedia initiative the Bloggers' Brunch (now Australia's premier influencer marketing event), spearheaded industry research assignment, called Australian Mums Today to understand what and why mums buy, and established S.M.A.R.T. business growth systems that take B2C relationships and revenue to a new level.

Along the way I wrote a book called The Mum Who Roared to motivate Mums to reclaim themselves as individuals, consistently been featured in media as the industry spokesperson, and won numerous awards, including Australian Women's Small Business Champion Awards.

I've always known success is about building relationships. My parents ran cafes so growing up I learned the art of connecting. After a derailed foray into my dream career as a news reporter, I took my fascination with people down a marketing path and worked with top entrepreneurs. It inspired me to create Mumpower.

Away from work, I run, enrolinaton of courses and spend quality time with family and friends to stay energised with life. Oh, and I once talked my way into meeting US President Bill Clinton. That taught me confidence and bravado pays, in business and in life.

BE UNAPOLOGETICALLY YOU

(UNLESS YOU STEAL OFFICE LUNCHES, THEN APOLOGISE)

DR CHELA CHOMICKI

It felt like my heart was pounding against the walls of my chest. I shrank down in my desk and closed my eyes, hoping that would make me invisible as I heard that dreaded, notorious question teachers enthusiastically ask at the beginning of every school year:

'What did you do this summer?'

You see, I was part of a Milwaukee program in the eighties called *Chapter 220*. It aimed to integrate schools by bussing dozens of poor inner-city minority students to middle-class white suburban schools. Milwaukee, at times, had been ranked the second most segregated city in the US. The program was created in 1975, after a federal judge found that the Milwaukee school district was *intentionally* segregating schools.

So, there I sat, surrounded by classmates who had spent their summers in olive-filled Italy, while I had visited the cotton fields of Mississippi.

They had recreation rooms and were encouraged to play inside. We better not play inside – we played outside.

They ate spaghetti for a snack. That *was* our meal.

They talked about investing in stocks and hedge funds. My friends talked about investing in the latest Jordans.

At first, the differences between us seemed like disadvantages; no trust funds, no stock options, no bougie summer vacations. But as I've travelled and grown, I've realised my background gave me something far more valuable than a yacht trip to Santorini – I had grit, adaptability and an advanced degree in making things happen. I was a bridge between two worlds, learning to navigate cultural differences, develop effective communication skills and master the fine art of code-switching before I even knew what that meant.

Instead of feeling embarrassed, I learned to embrace my background. I couldn't always relate to my classmates, so I became an excellent listener (and a strategic eavesdropper, especially when they talked about stocks). I got comfortable with myself. I wasn't deprived. The rich kids had portfolios, but I had *hustle*. I mastered creative problem-solving, like stretching a dollar as if it was an Olympic sport.

My background wasn't a weakness – it was my superpower. I learned resilience, resourcefulness and how to navigate spaces where I was often not expected to belong. These gifts continued to help me throughout my life from the streets to the boardrooms. I could not underestimate the power of street smarts and creative problem-solving. Book smarts are great, but knowing how to navigate life when things aren't handed to you? Priceless. Street smarts and book smarts combined? *Unstoppable*.

Let me show you what I mean.

Problem: I had to figure out how to pay for college. Solution: Sell educational books door to door in New Hampshire, where 0.73% of the population identified as Black or African American.

I saw a flyer promising I could make enough to pay for college in one summer. My friends thought I was crazy, and they were convinced that I'd get kidnapped. But I signed up, went to Tennessee for sales training, and then got shipped off to New Hampshire to sell books door to door.

AUTHENTICITY & ACTION

Before each house, I would psych myself up by saying: *Chela, you are a drop-dead sexy bookseller. Everybody wants your books. Everybody is buying them.* That summer, as I pedalled around on a little kid's bike, I had doors slammed in my face, police called on me and dogs sicced on me. However, I learned the power of a positive attitude, positive self-talk and, more importantly, that people can smell fake from a mile away. Forced enthusiasm? Fake humility? They see right through it. Be real or prepare for awkward silences and no sales.

Oh, and another lesson? Being cheap can be expensive. I needed a car to deliver my books to my customers. I tried to save money by buying a $200 car with a manual transmission that I didn't know how to drive. It caught on fire at a tollbooth. Did I worry about my life? No. I worried about getting my books out before they burned because I couldn't afford to replace them. Priorities.

Eventually, I did figure out a way to get my books delivered, and just in case you're wondering, I made enough money to pay for half of a semester. Sometimes taking action means messing up. Fail fast, learn faster. Bonus points if your failures make for a great dinner-party story.

Problem: I wanted to travel the world but had no money. (Read: made less than $15,000 a year.)

Solution: Find research programs and sponsors to fund my adventures.

By the time I finished my master's degree, I had travelled to almost forty countries without going into debt. How? I stopped trying to 'balance' my passions and started *integrating* them. I leveraged every available resource at my disposal.

Case in point: my externship in South Africa. I had seen an Oprah special where she gave away shoes to kids, and I felt *called* to help. But I had no contacts, no money and no solid plan. So, I did what I had been trained to do – I knocked on doors.

First, I asked my department. *No money.* Then, I saw that my university's president was the second-highest-paid in the country. *Bingo.* I scheduled a meeting.

I nervously explained my passion for helping South African youth, particularly those who were HIV infected and affected. By the end of our conversation, he had pledged his support. He connected me with a professor, Dr Norma Gaines-Hanks who helped set up my externship at the Mohau Centre, an HIV/AIDS orphanage, where I lived and worked with the children, ran a support group for HIV-infected women and joined community health workers when they went out to provide basic medicine in the informal settlements.

When other organisations heard that the *president* had backed me, they suddenly found money, too. Lesson? Money attracts money, or as my husband says, 'Money is only friends with other money.'

When I returned to tell the president I no longer needed his money, he laughed and funded my follow-up research trip six months later. Sometimes, support is more valuable than a cheque.

The world is full of people who *plan* to do things. Be the one who actually *does* them. Less talking, more action! Don't just talk about it – be about it! Encourage anyone with a dream who may feel ill-equipped and unprepared to not quit. Someone needs what you have. You could be just one meeting away from connecting with the person who could help you fulfill your dream. We all have the power to help someone else.

Problem: I needed a full-time job but had no contacts in a new city. Solution: Build a network from scratch through informational interviews (and a little charm).

I was told that if I wanted to work in health disparities, I *had* to meet Dr Steve Whitman. He was an Ivy League epidemiologist who built a community health research institute to combat the greatest disparities that plagued the inner city of Chicago. I called him. He invited me to a hospital cafeteria for a tuna sandwich. I told him I don't eat tuna but

AUTHENTICITY & ACTION

would gladly *watch* him eat tuna. That was the beginning of our fantastic (and fishy) friendship. By the end of the meeting, he offered me a job.

The work was intense. We had to convince uninsured, underinsured and sometimes undocumented women to get mammograms and follow up with diagnostic mammograms and cancer treatment. At the time, in Chicago, white women got breast cancer more, but Black women and Latinas died more. We got creative; mammogram parties with salsa dancing lessons, fashion shows and door-to-door outreach. We would even pick people up to take them to their doctor's appointments. Once, I had to pick up a little old Mexican lady for an appointment. Based on my Spanish over the phone, she thought I was Latina. When she saw me, she hesitated to even come out of her house to get in my car so I could take her to her doctor's appointment. Once I proved I was *Chela*, we laughed the whole ride there.

I wasn't offended. I realised that this was just another problem I needed to creatively solve. Lesson? Like death and taxes, problems and misunderstandings are inevitable. The better you get at not getting frustrated (or as my three-year-old used to say, 'not getting flusterated'), the better your quality of life will be.

Being a door-to-door salesperson was one of the hardest things I've ever done, but I've been knocking on doors ever since – sometimes figuratively, sometimes literally.

The lessons I learned from door knocking have aided me throughout my life. I have continued to have to knock on doors or knock them down. I see setbacks as rocket fuel for my future. Whether it is rejection, disappointment or heartbreak, I use it all to fuel my future. I don't put limitations on my dreams. In fact, I increase my expectations and guard my big dreams from small-minded people. Lastly, I learned that my greatest asset is not my financial capital but my social capital; relationships are one of the biggest superpowers of success.

DR CHELA CHOMICKI

At the end of the day, nobody cares where you spent your summer – they care about who you became. Your experiences, no matter how different make you uniquely you. Whether you summered in Europe or summered on your grandma's porch in Mississippi, you've got something valuable to bring to the table.

And that's exactly what I want you to do – pull up a chair. The world needs your voice, your hustle and your authenticity. There's no assigned seating in this life, so don't wait for permission. Take action. Be bold. Be unapologetically you. And as Shirley Chisholm, the first African American woman elected to the US Congress says, *'If they don't give you a seat at the table, bring a folding chair.'* You belong there.

DR CHELA CHOMICKI

Dr. Chela Chomicki's journey is one of resilience, passion, and purpose. She has gone from knocking on doors as a determined bookseller to opening doors of opportunity for others through leadership, education, and advocacy. Her career spans community health education to executive leadership, always with a focus on empowering individuals, families, and organizations to thrive.

With a deep commitment to social impact, Dr. Chela has conducted research and service in over 100 countries and across the U.S., addressing health disparities, cultural inclusion, and leadership development. She holds a Ph.D. in Human Ecology with a concentration in Health Disparities in the Latino and African Diaspora, a Master's in Public Administration, and a Bachelor's in Spanish and Business Administration. A lifelong advocate for marginalized communities, she leads with both lived experience and academic expertise, understanding firsthand what it means to overcome disenfranchisement.

As President & CEO of CC Strategic Solutions, Dr. Chela is at the forefront of leadership transformation, equipping executives and organizations with the strategies, cultural intelligence, and global perspective needed to thrive in an evolving world. Her firm specializes in developing

DR CHELA CHOMICKI

high-impact leaders, strengthening organizational culture, and fostering inclusive workplaces that drive innovation and performance. Through executive coaching, immersive leadership training, and dynamic cultural intelligence programs, CC Strategic Solutions empowers organizations to build resilient, forward-thinking leaders who can navigate complexity with confidence and authenticity.

And she's doing all of this while traveling the world—encouraging leaders to rediscover their joy, passion, and purpose through immersive travel and cultural exploration. Whether solo or in curated group experiences, Dr. Chela transports leaders beyond the boardroom, helping them gain fresh perspectives, challenge assumptions, and return with renewed vision and clarity. By bridging cultures and perspectives, she helps companies unlock new opportunities, enhance team dynamics, and lead with purpose on a global scale.

Dr. Chela's impact has been recognized with numerous prestigious awards, including:

- Named one of the "BPM Global 100 Leading Black Professionals" by ICABA
- Winner of the S.H.I.N.E. Speaker Showcase competition with Justin Guarini
- 2025 Women Changing the World first place winner of Women in Travel Retreats and Events and second place winner in Culture, Diversity and Inclusion categories.
- TEDxMcAllen Finalist

Her expertise has also led her to national and regional speaking engagements, including at Westchester University, Cal Poly Humboldt, Colorado State University, and the Andersonville Chamber of Commerce. She is a proud graduate of the Cornell University Institute for Women's

AUTHENTICITY & ACTION

Entrepreneurship, the Polsky Small Business Financial Fundamentals program, and the Inner City Capital Connections program, further strengthening her ability to drive change at the intersection of business, leadership, and social impact.

Through every chapter of her career, Dr. Chela remains steadfast in her mission: to develop bold, purpose-driven leaders, build high-impact businesses, and drive meaningful social change. Whether in the boardroom or across the globe, Dr. Chela is dedicated to empowering leaders to break barriers, create inclusive workplaces, and build businesses that don't just succeed—but make a difference.

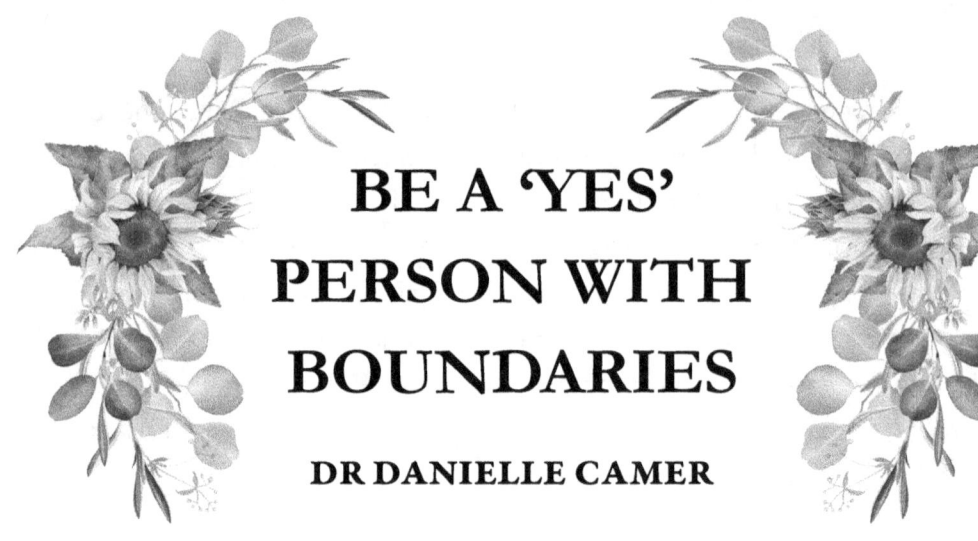

BE A 'YES' PERSON WITH BOUNDARIES

DR DANIELLE CAMER

I was a "yes" person without boundaries:

Yes, I will do more work for no extra pay.

Yes, I will stay up late after my baby goes to sleep so I can get that project to you ASAP even though I'm exhausted.

Yes, I will work through lunch to meet your arbitrary deadline.

My perspective changed after a serious car accident that almost claimed my life. I made the switch to be a "YES" person with boundaries.

THE RED FLAG

I went back to work after a short maternity leave when my daughter was around four months old. Juggling work with family life was hard. The three- four-hour daily work commutes, the daycare sicknesses, the late nights, managing living with Crohn's disease, making time for family and date nights, were just a few things that were difficult to navigate.

I was scared of losing the reputation I had built throughout my career in advertising, as the high performing perfectionist writer with exceptional attention to detail, who would always put work first and aim to please. A "YES" person to my core. I was determined to keep climbing the ladder at all costs. I was exceeding my KPIs, training new employees,

AUTHENTICITY & ACTION

had a glowing reputation with clients, and was working way above my pay grade and level.

Months after returning to work from maternity leave, I mustered up the courage to request my long-overdue promotion, for the role I was already doing. I prepared hard and met with my manager for my performance review. I received a response along the lines of, *"You can't get a promotion because you have health issues and family responsibilities."*

This should have been a big red flag. I was angry. I was upset. I cried many tears. But most of all, I felt undervalued. I knew I would always be a mother and have Crohn's disease, but would this really mean the end of advancing in my career? Would I be stuck at the same level forever? The glass ceiling felt like it was made of concrete, peppered with barbed wire and jagged diamonds.

I did eventually get the promotion, but the comment stayed with me. I knew that whatever I would do, I wouldn't feel good enough, even though I was working harder than ever.

Spot the red flags.
Is someone making you feel undervalued in any part of your life?
Trust your gut. If something doesn't seem right, it most likely isn't.

THE TURNING POINT

Everything changed on the 14th April 2018. The wake-up call I needed, started with my very near death.

It was time for a girls trip with my three soul sisters/best friends. We were excited for a day together exploring wineries around the South Coast in NSW, Australia. We were going to frolic in our pretty dresses in the outdoors and take those classic BFF selfies in front of picturesque vines and hills. At our first winery, we did that and more. We took the photo, ate some cheese and bought more wine than we were supposed to for our first stop.

Back on the highway, as "Sweet Nothing" by Calvin Harris played in the background, we waited to make a turn into our second destination. But we never made it. In a split millisecond, that seemed like slow motion, my senses experienced something I had never experienced before. A whole movie reel playing glimpses of my life flickered in front of me as vivid memories. I heard what sounded like a jumbo jet engine, along with the sound of a dozen waiters dropping trays of glasses right behind me. I smelt the fresh country air that travelled freely from the glassless windows coupled with essence of tyres. I tasted the roof of my mouth. I felt numb but in pain at the same time. Then, I opened my eyes.

Although I was originally sat on the left passenger seat, I was suddenly positioned in the middle seat, with my seatbelt still tightly secured. My view was of stopped oncoming traffic - 180 degrees from where we started. And definitely not where we were supposed to be.

The girls screamed. I remained calm and silent, crab walking across the seat and out the right door, keeping my head very still. I saw the car that had rear-ended us in a ditch. The other, which we'd side swiped after our car spun, was in the middle of the road. My friends wondered how I fit into the crushed space that had been my seat, in the soon to be written off hatchback. I was glad we were all conscious and alive.

Still calm, and most definitely concussed, I consoled the others. I called my husband to let him know what had happened and to tell him we were all OK. Concerned, he asked if the car was drivable. I remember saying an elongated, "Nooooooo!" He later told me that he knew, at that moment, this accident was more serious than I was telling him. I reassured him we were getting a lift to take us home and we were all fine, or so I thought.

Suddenly dizziness overcame me. My head was stinging. As the pain

AUTHENTICITY & ACTION

kept travelling around my head and neck, the paramedics swiftly put me in a neck brace before loading me up into an ambulance.

I always knew that these girls were my people, but this day made us even closer. They stayed by my side.

Everyone who interacted with me kept saying, "Wow, you are so lucky to be alive!" I really understood why they were saying this and was very grateful, but this comment made me feel so uneasy.

I was scanned from head to toe, poked and prodded with needles, and stared at my only view of the ceiling. It started to get late and my friends went home, as I was admitted overnight. My husband said he would come to see me and bring our daughter, but I didn't want them to travel on the road that had almost killed me and told them to stay home. I was in a hospital that was around two hours away from home. Lonely and scared, I couldn't sleep. I was replaying what happened over and over in my head.

I was eventually transferred to my local hospital for further investigations under a neurosurgeon. After briefly being discharged, I was urgently called back in, after the team had spotted something serious that needed critical review. On my scan, they had noticed a dissection of my left vertebral artery, a critical artery in the neck. If I'd had just a millimetre of more damage, I would have died instantly. There was a high risk of me having a stroke, so I was taken straight to the stroke ward for more testing.

As I lay in the stroke ward in hospital, my first thoughts were, *"When will I be able to go back to work?", "I better email my boss soon, so he doesn't think I'm being unreliable," "Will I get demoted since I can't deliver my deadlines?"*

At 30 years old, I WAS IN THE STROKE WARD, because I was at risk of having a stroke since I had dissected a vital artery in my neck. But for some reason, I was more worried about work.

I sent an email updating my manager that I was back in hospital and currently in the stroke ward, reassuring him I would keep him updated about when I will be able to return to work. The reply I received was, *"OK thanks."* I realised just how dispensable I was at work. I needed to make a move to something better.

Live your life. Do what you want to do now.
You never know what is around the corner.

HEALING AND GROWTH

One day, I decided I wanted to visit the winery we never made it to that day, for some exposure therapy. As my husband drove closer to the road, my breathing was heavy and my heart was racing. I closed my eyes, then my husband said, "Wait, it's a new road! The one you were on is not there anymore!" I sighed with relief that a new stretch of road, with a turning bay for improved safety, now existed.

I was lucky to meet the wonderful owner while I was there. I started to panic and began sobbing. I told him about my accident, and he knew exactly which one it was. He told me that the accident I was in was the reason they were able to finally get approval for a safer road with a turning bay. The community had campaigned for years with no luck, even after many previous fatalities at that spot. It was such a special moment to know that positive change happened after such a traumatic event.

He also shared with me his own traumatic experience of losing staff in the 9/11 terror attack in NYC and that this was the catalyst to move to Australia and run a winery with his family. It was early days in my own trauma, but this gave me the hope I needed and reassurance that things would be OK.

Find the one positive in a million negatives.
There is always hope.

AUTHENTICITY & ACTION

THE REBOUND

I searched for a workplace where I would feel valued, beginning the process of being a "YES" person with some boundaries.

Before accepting a position in a new workplace, I was upfront that I had a family, Crohn's disease, was recently diagnosed with PTSD from a serious car accident, had to see many healthcare professionals, and could only work part-time. My next employer agreed with my boundaries and things started off well.

At two-years-old, my daughter was now in daycare more often and at the peak of taking every disease from daycare home. I was on an immunosuppressant drug to help with the management of Crohn's disease, which would make me pick up every germ. I was also attending several specialist, psychology and physiology appointments to help manage my injuries from the car accident.

I had maxed my sick leave, so I would turn up to the office sick.

Then an unsolicited comment came from a manager; *"You're always sick. You're like a walking petri dish."* He thought he was so funny. I was raging inside. I was frustrated with my health. I never asked to be sick. I was immunocompromised and it was something I could not control.

One day, a manager pulled me into the office kitchen for a chat. He lectured me, the crux of the conversation being *me not wanting to work many extra hours*. "We are an agency, and as such, are expected to work like we are in an agency, including being expected to work until midnight and even sleep on the floor." I was dumbfounded.

I felt incredibly stressed and humiliated. I was working my contracted hours plus more, but *the more* wasn't enough. I was already spinning so many plates in my life and couldn't give more time to work for free. I was left with that feeling of inadequacy again. Being a "YES" person with boundaries was not going to work here. I needed to find another solution.

You might accidently miss a red flag at first. Mistakes happen. Try again.

Don't let anyone undervalue or humiliate you.

REMEMBERING MY WORTH

The best way to have a clear head is to travel somewhere else. I had left yet another workplace and was on route to a family trip to the UK. I would spend quality time with my family and then figure out my next career move when I got back.

Since the accident, we lived the time we had together as a family to the full. The Savoy Hotel in London had a themed afternoon tea of my daughter's favourite book at the time, "The Tiger Who Came to Tea" by Judith Kerr, so we planned to visit for the day. We also booked a stay there overnight for a treat too.

At check in, I was told we had been upgraded to one of the hotel's luxurious personality suites, which came with our own personal butler. I was excited, but I had a thought that I wasn't worthy of this level of treatment. I had been so undervalued by others, it had really affected my confidence.

I watched as my two-year-old daughter walked past the opulent vases and marble in our room and straight to the enticing bowl of fresh fruit, grabbing a strawberry and devouring it like a toddler would. No fear, no worry. She made the most of the experience by seizing an opportunity. I wanted that confidence.

As it was an overnight stay, we had only taken a small bag with us, leaving our main luggage with family. I forgot to pack an extra pair of socks to wear for the next day. Usually, I would have dealt with the mild discomfort of wearing boots without socks, but I remembered the room came with a butler service. Inspired by my daughter's courage, I called the butler and requested a pair of socks. A short time later, a pair of socks

AUTHENTICITY & ACTION

wrapped in a bow arrived. I was so grateful.

You are worthy.
Enjoy your gifts and wins. Embrace opportunities.

WORKING FOR ME

After returning from my family trip to the UK in 2019, I committed to starting a freelance medical writing business from home. I researched, completed courses, joined networking groups, contacted potential clients – anything I could to make sure I was setting up my business for success, on my own terms. My own workplace, where I could be the "YES" person with boundaries.

I continue to be committed to having work-life balance, where I can have more time for my family and health, and only work with others who are aligned with my values. I'm not afraid to walk away from red flags. I won't allow others to undervalue me.

Find your dream workplace.
The grass IS greener on the other side.

ALLOWING TIME FOR CREATIVITY

With more time to breathe, the flexibility of having my own freelance medical writing business allowed me to pursue a creative outlet on the side – writing children's picture books.

I was inspired by my daughter to self-publish my first children's picture book, *Sophie Won't Sleep*. Since its release on 1st December 2021, *Sophie Won't Sleep* has achieved global success, including receiving ten prestigious international picture book awards, and featuring on a billboard in Times Square, NYC. I have since received publishing contracts for more picture books, including, *Squirrel Takes the Cake*, which was published in

2024, and *That Doesn't Go!* which is due for release in 2025/2026.

This is a path I had never originally planned to take in my career, but I'm so glad I did. It gives me so much joy to see how much happiness these stories bring to other children, especially my daughter.

Are you inspired to do something else?
Find a way to make it happen

It hasn't always been an easy path, but I am proud to be a "YES" person with boundaries. I hope sharing my story will inspire you to grab opportunities with open arms, but only if they align with your values. Live life to the full, but within your comfort levels. Don't let anyone make you be anyone else but you.

Dedication: To Mum and Dad – Thank you for your support with opportunities I take in life. To my soul sisters (Jenny, Courtney, and Beth) – Thanks for being the best friends I could ever have in my life. To my husband, Clint – I'm so grateful we lived and loved life together to the full, right until the end of your short 37 years of life. To Sophie – You make the world shine by being you. Don't let anyone break your confidence.

DR DANIELLE CAMER

Dr Danielle Camer is a leading Australian Senior Medical Writer, Creative Director and multi-award-winning Children's Picture Book Author. With passions for medicine and creativity, her university education encompasses a Bachelor of Creative Arts (with Distinction), Bachelor of Medical Science Hons (Class I) and a PhD in Neuroscience (with Examiners' commendation for outstanding thesis). She has previous careers in medical research and university teaching, has presented at leading national and international conferences, been published in international journals, and received several awards for outstanding teaching and academic performance.

After returning to work at a medical advertising agency from maternity leave in 2017, Danielle was tired of commuting 3–4 hours a day, where she would leave home at 6 am and not return until 7:30/8 pm. Her husband was doing the daycare drop-offs and pick-ups and Danielle felt she was missing out on precious time with her daughter and forming connections with daycare educators. This led to her starting her freelance medical writing business from home in 2019. This flexibility also allowed her to pursue a creative outlet on the side – writing children's picture books!

Danielle was inspired by her daughter, Sophie, to write her first picture book, "Sophie Won't Sleep". The main plot of the story is that it's bedtime for Sophie sloth! But she wants treetop adventures instead. Will Sophie *ever* make it to bed? Before it was a book, Danielle would perform the story to Sophie with her husband using sloth toys. From when she was 2 years old, Sophie kept asking when "Sophie Won't Sleep" would become an actual book that she could keep on her bookshelf. Danielle was determined to make this dream a reality.

After many late nights, research, courses, and determination, Danielle published her first children's picture book, "Sophie Won't Sleep" on 1st December 2021. Since its publication, "Sophie Won't Sleep", has achieved global success, receiving 10 prestigious international book awards, including a Gold Medal in the 2023 Moonbeam Children's Book Awards, and has featured on a billboard in Times Square, NYC. In 2024, Danielle also received the AusMumpreneur Silver Author of the Year Award and was listed as one of the global 40 under 40 in publishing at BookCAMP USA, recognising her outstanding contribution to all aspects of authorship and excellence in publishing.

Exactly 2 years after Danielle published "Sophie Won't Sleep", her husband, Clint, tragically died from a rare and aggressive cancer (metastatic melanoma) aged 37 on 1st December 2023. Danielle is a single parent to their 7-year-old, Sophie, who inspired her to start a career as a picture book author and provides the drive to live the life that Clint can no longer have to the full. With this determination behind her, Danielle released her second picture book, "Squirrel Takes the Cake" in August 2024 and has publishing contracts for more. This includes her third picture book in 2025/2026, "That Doesn't Go!", which is co-written with Sophie, and is based on an idea by Clint.

Instagram: https://www.instagram.com/drdaniellecamer/
Facebook: https://www.facebook.com/drdaniellecamer
LinkedIn: https://www.linkedin.com/in/daniellecamer/

AUTHENTICITY & ACTION

Website: https://www.daniellecamer.com.au

Donate to Melanoma Institute Australia: https://inmemory.melanoma.org.au/page/ClintEdwardShumack

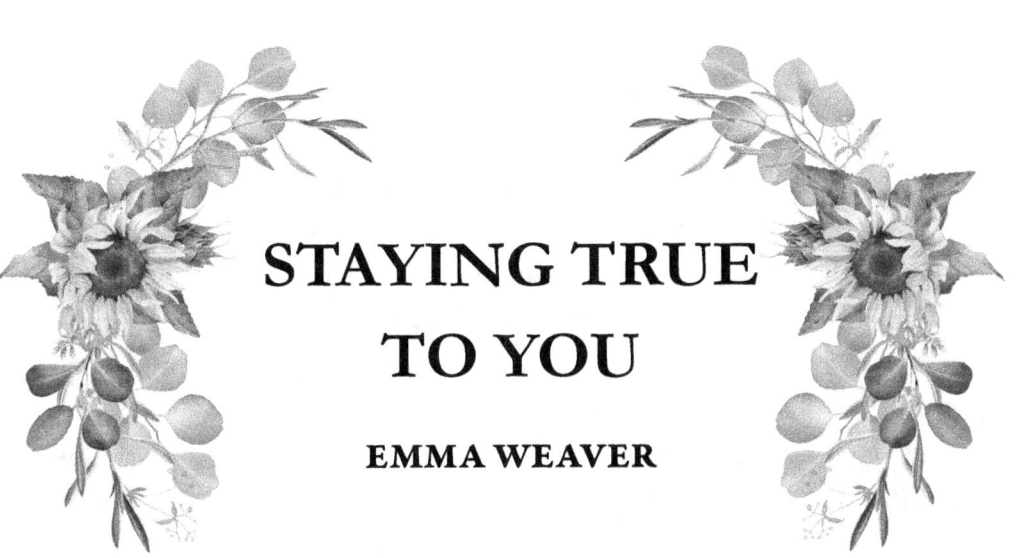

STAYING TRUE TO YOU

EMMA WEAVER

Life has a way of throwing unexpected challenges our way, but with determination, resilience and grit, we can succeed in anything we put our minds to and take action on. Success can only be defined on your terms, so it's important to take stock of what success looks like to you, write it down, and work it backwards. My journey is no exception and through every challenge, I have come to understand the true power of authenticity and action.

As a young mother, I found myself facing the responsibilities of parenthood at an age when most of my peers were still exploring their own paths. Balancing the demands of motherhood while pursuing education was no easy feat. My call to education came from a deep knowing that it could change my fate. I knew I had to take action, even small steps in the right direction making a difference. Many believed that getting pregnant so young meant my life was over, but I had a desire to change the narrative, to create a life beyond the poverty trap, judgemental family and limiting expectations. This was by no means easy, and I didn't do it alone. I received support along the journey, but my commitment to providing a better life for my child fuelled my determination. I set an intention to create a new path and, in doing so, gained valuable lessons in time management, sacrifice and the power of setting priorities.

I graduated on 11 September 2001 – a day known for many other reasons, however, for me, it was the day I gifted myself and my daughter a better future. Today, she is an accomplished doctor of psychology, a testament to the power of perseverance. I now have three wonderful children, each forging their own paths. Education was the key to unlocking new possibilities, but my journey didn't stop there.

Upon entering the workforce, I discovered my true calling; mental health advocacy allowed me to show up authentically in the world. Supporting people to live independently, create fulfilling lives and maintain their wellbeing became my mission. With a heart full of empathy, understanding and a deep desire to make a difference, I embarked on a journey that would span over two decades. I worked my way up into management, seizing every opportunity that aligned with my purpose and allowed me to stay true to myself. One lesson I learned early on was to never let an opportunity pass by. Be persistent, have courage and trust that you will figure things out. It has been a guiding principle to simply show up, be confident and have faith in the process. 'Control the controllables' became an affirmation I frequently used to navigate challenges.

This journey was not without its trials. I faced many personal struggles which tested my resilience, but each moment of darkness strengthened my resolve and deepened my empathy. Along the way, I sought understanding, not just in the world around me, but within myself. Learning to meditate and journal became part of my daily routine. These were not practices I had been shown growing up, but I knew they would make a difference, strengthen my mind and, ultimately, teach me to trust myself. Trusting myself took time, as I had spent so long consumed by the opinions of others, constantly caregiving and seeking external validation. But through doing the internal work, I stepped into my authenticity, fully embracing my own definition of success.

AUTHENTICITY & ACTION

One of the most profound realisations I had was understanding the impact of limiting beliefs. Sometimes, these beliefs are not even our own; they are societal constructs that dictate what we should or shouldn't do based on gender, background or circumstance. As a young mother and later as a woman in leadership, I had to break through these invisible barriers and recognise that the only limits that truly exist are the ones we accept. This was a turning point in my journey – understanding that if I wanted to create change, I needed to take radical responsibility for my own mindset and actions.

When I understood that overcoming adversity isn't just about pushing through, it's about finding the lessons, growth and inner strength that come from those experiences, it was life changing. I realised authenticity is not just about being true to oneself but about taking action that aligns with your truth.

Driven by my passion for mental health and fuelled by a defining moment at Crom Castle, an event my sister had founded bringing together like-minded people from across the globe, I decided to take a leap of faith. A single talk at the event stood out, sparking a realisation within me; I had never previously considered leaving my job to create my own organisation. However, two weeks after the event, I awoke in the middle of the night with a flood of ideas. I grabbed the notebook I always kept beside my bed and started writing. The thoughts kept flowing, and from that moment, Mental Wealth International was born.

This was more than just a business venture, it was a calling that would not leave me. I knew I had to take action. With definiteness of purpose and a clear plan, I had to choose courage every step of the way. The road was filled with challenges; funding, resources and logistical hurdles tested my resolve. But each obstacle reaffirmed that success is not a linear path, it is a series of twists and turns requiring adaptability and perseverance.

A key lesson in leadership and business is clarity. I had to get crystal clear on my goals and constantly ask myself, *Is this decision taking me closer to my goal?* When faced with difficult choices, I learned to trust my intuition and measure each decision against my vision. Not all opportunities are meant for you, and learning to discern what aligns with your purpose is just as important as taking action.

As we built Mental Wealth International, I understood that the foundation extended beyond strategies and business plans. It was built on an unwavering commitment to mental health, a passion for creating positive change and a belief that workplaces must prioritise their employees' wellbeing. Leading by example became crucial. I practiced self-care, pursued continuous learning and ensured that my own mental wealth was prioritised.

Mental Wealth International transformed from an idea into a movement, globally impacting lives and workplaces. I had learned that when aligned opportunities present themselves, it takes courage to say yes. As my sister Karen always says, 'If it's not a hell yes, it's a definite no.' Following this guidance led me to experiences I had never envisioned, including delivering two TEDx talks – one inspired by my book *The Blue Line* about my journey through IVF; the other focused on Mental Wealth, my true calling. These experiences reaffirmed the power of using my voice and supporting others in doing the same.

A defining moment in my journey was participating in the *Seven Levels Deep* exercise – a simple yet impactful activity that helps uncover the true 'why' behind our actions. It made me realise that my deepest motivation was to help others find and use their voice, because there was a time when I felt unheard. Becoming pregnant at a young age in a small Irish community meant losing my voice – for a while, anyway – but through resilience, self-discovery and action, I reclaimed it. This realisation led me to apply for a TEDx license, creating opportunities for others to share their ideas with the world. Curating two TEDx events

AUTHENTICITY & ACTION

and supporting others to create impact has been one of my proudest achievements.

All of these experiences have shaped me into the confident, competent leader I am today, showing up authentically, being of service and living a life by design. The success of Mental Wealth International has strengthened my ongoing commitment to making a lasting impact. Every success is a collective effort, shaped by the contributions of a passionate team, supportive networks and those who believe in the power of mental wellbeing.

This success has led to other business ventures in Cynestx and now MWI publishing. These are also aligned with my purpose to support others to have their voice heard in the business world and the written word. Life has a beautiful way of guiding you down different paths and we get *to choose* which to take. As mentioned earlier, it's so important to have a goal, a clear intention, and every time, ask yourself if this opportunity will take you closer to your goal. If it's a *hell yes* then go with it and if it's an *I don't know* or a *no* – it's simply a *NO*. It's important, for women in particular, to recognise that NO is a full sentence. We will often say yes to things when really we want to say no. This is a way of not being true to ourselves and we sometimes need to work on this, but honestly, it's the best thing you can do for yourself. And the more you do it, the easier it gets.

Remember, the journey to success is not about personal accolades, it's about lives transformed, conversations ignited and the ripple effect of positive change. Through authenticity and action, we create the life we were meant to live.

EMMA WEAVER

Emma Weaver is a thought leader in the industry of mental wealth, dedicating over two decades to empowering individuals and organisations worldwide to prioritise mental well-being. As the founder of Mental Wealth International, Emma's visionary leadership drives initiatives that foster resilience and growth.

With a diverse background spanning entrepreneurship, public speaking, and event curation, Emma has become a respected keynote speaker and MC, captivating audiences across the globe. Her dynamic presence on the TEDx stage, where she has been invited twice, underscores her ability to challenge perceptions and spark crucial conversations about mental health and wellness. As the curator of TEDx Enniskillen, Emma has orchestrated two highly successful events, cultivating a community committed to sharing ideas for positive change. Her global reach extends beyond TEDx, as she is sought after for her engaging presentations on business development, global expansion, resilience, and personal growth. From Dubai to Los Angeles, Emma's expertise and perspective enrich every stage she graces.

In addition to her speaking engagements, Emma is a bestselling author, with her debut novel "The Blue Line" and co-author of numerous

EMMA WEAVER

books, including her latest work "Mental Wealth". A successful businesswoman, Emma mentors and supports ecommerce ventures and a diverse range of businesses, striving to unlock their full potential. Emma now owns MWI publishing, a publishing company supporting authors to write their stories and create impact in the world.

Driven by a passion to create a world where mental well-being is celebrated and prioritized, Emma leverages her platform to advocate for positive change. Through her various endeavors, she continues to inspire individuals to thrive in all aspects of life, embodying the ethos of mental wealth.

FROM LOVE, FINDING PURPOSE, CREATING CHANGE

HAYLEY BOSWELL

Many people know that my life is devoted to creating positive change, but only a few truly understand how it all began … and why. In the early days, I couldn't have imagined that a simple idea, born from love and determination, would grow into something that would touch so many lives. It started as a small seed, a quiet hope, and an unwavering desire to make a difference. At the time, I had no way of knowing that this little idea would transform into something so meaningful; something that empowers, heals and builds futures. Looking back now, I'm overwhelmed with gratitude and humility for all it has become.

Whenever someone asks me how it started, my answer is always the same; love. Love was the spark, the foundation and the force behind every decision I made. It was my love for family, the community and the people who sacrifice so much, that drove me forward. Love became my guide when everything felt uncertain. It gave me strength when I felt weak, clarity when I felt lost, and hope when the path ahead seemed impossible to navigate.

But love alone wasn't enough. I realised that staying true to myself, even when the challenges seemed overwhelming, was just as important.

Authenticity became my anchor. For me, authenticity means embracing the messy, imperfect parts of life and showing up with your whole heart. It's about being honest with the world about who you are, even when that honesty feels vulnerable. Staying authentic allowed me to create something real and lasting - something that could truly make a difference.

This chapter isn't just about how it all began, it's about the power of starting small, leading with love and staying true to yourself, even in the face of uncertainty. It's about planting a seed and believing, against all odds, that it will grow into something extraordinary.

Many still think that what I've created was part of an elaborate plan on which I had brainstormed for months. The truth couldn't be further from that. This journey didn't begin with a detailed blueprint or a clear vision. It started, years ago, when I was trying to figure out who I was and what I wanted to do with my life. For many of us, this is a relatable situation; knowing you have potential but not quite knowing how to channel it. I was living in suburban Adelaide, searching for meaning and yearning for something that felt significant.

Everything changed the day I met Bradley.

Bradley wasn't the kind of person who turned heads in a room, but there was something about him that left a mark on everyone he met. He had a quiet confidence; the kind that comes from being comfortable in your own skin. Bradley didn't try to impress anyone, and yet, he had a way of making everyone around him feel important. His kindness was genuine and it was the type of kindness that made you want to be a better person.

Spending time with Bradley was refreshing. He didn't pretend to be something he wasn't, and that authenticity drew me to him. Being with him made me realise I didn't need to have everything figured out to make a difference. I didn't need to be perfect or have all the answers. I just needed to be myself, to be present and to trust that who I was - and

AUTHENTICITY & ACTION

who I was becoming - was enough. That realisation stayed with me and changed the way I approached life.

Bradley and I became inseparable almost from the moment we met. Our weekends were filled with movie marathons, laughter and deep conversations about everything and nothing. For the first time in my life, I felt truly seen. Bradley had a way of making all the messy, disconnected parts of me feel like they fit together perfectly.

But then, when we were seventeen, everything shifted. Life took an unexpected turn, and Bradley joined the Royal Australian Navy. I still remember the day he told me. He was excited, his eyes full of hope, but all I could feel was a sinking sense of loss. My best friend, my anchor, was leaving. When he left Adelaide, my world felt smaller, quieter and lonelier.

At first, I tried to distract myself. I buried myself in school, took on extra assignments and juggled a part-time job to stay busy. But no matter how packed my schedule got, I couldn't shake the emptiness his absence created. I missed everything about him; the way he could make me laugh on my worst days, our long talks about life and the understanding we shared without ever needing to explain ourselves.

Despite the distance, I held onto hope. I didn't know when or how, but I believed our story wasn't over.

In the years that followed, I began carving out my own path. I became a youth worker, dedicating my time to helping children who had been disengaged from school or removed from their families. This work opened my eyes in ways I never expected. The resilience these kids displayed, despite the hardships they faced, inspired me every day. Watching them find hope and strength became my purpose. It felt meaningful, like I was doing something that mattered.

Later, I decided to take another leap and enrolled in law school, later specialising in human rights. Becoming a lawyer felt like the right next step. My passion was representing women who had been mistreated in the workplace by helping them reclaim their voices and their dignity. The work was fulfilling and rewarding; I felt proud of the difference I was making in the world. But even then, something felt incomplete. I kept asking myself, "Is this it? Is this all there is?"

The missing piece came back into my life when Bradley returned, years later. A simple message reconnected us, and from the moment we reunited, it was as if no time had passed. Soon enough, we welcomed our first beautiful daughter.

Becoming a mother changed me in ways I never could have anticipated. For the first time, everything in my life felt aligned. But as Bradley's deployments approached, I found myself grappling with how to explain his absences to Evie. How could I help her understand that her dad's time away wasn't about leaving, but about his commitment to something bigger, to protecting our country, our people, our wildlife?

When I searched for resources to help, I found nothing that truly addressed the unique challenges military families face. That realisation was a turning point. If no one else had created something like this, maybe I could.

So, I trusted the process. I took a leap of faith and allowed my passion to guide me. I wrote a simple, personalised picture book for our daughter, explaining Bradley's role in the Navy and why he sometimes had to be away. What started as a small project for my daughter quickly grew. Friends and family saw the book and asked for copies. Soon, military families from all over the country were reaching out, sharing their stories and expressing how much they needed *something like this*.

That's when I felt a shift deep within me, a clarity I had never experienced before. In my heart, I knew I had to give this my all. This was my purpose, my chance to create change and empower families like mine. It wasn't just about making tools for connection; it was about ensuring that

AUTHENTICITY & ACTION

every military family felt seen, heard and supported.

Encouraged by their response, I started creating more resources. Picture books, colouring sheets and interactive activities became tools to help military children feel understood and connected to their parents' service. It was no longer just a personal effort - it was growing into something that could make a real impact, including working with the government to advocate for positive policy change for military families.

Advocacy has always been at the heart of my journey. It's not just about raising awareness, it's about taking meaningful action to create lasting change. Advocacy gives a voice to those who often feel unheard, shining a light on the unique challenges faced by military families and empowering them to seek the support they deserve.

One of the proudest moments in this journey has been working with the South Australian Government to establish the first Veterans' Families Day in Australia. This day is a recognition of the sacrifices made, not just by those who serve in the military, but by the families who stand beside them through every deployment, relocation and homecoming. It's a day that acknowledges the resilience, love and unwavering support that bind these families together.

This achievement wasn't just about creating a day on the calendar, it was about fostering understanding and creating a platform for military families to share their stories. It was about ensuring they felt seen, valued and supported by their communities. Advocacy like this reminds us of the power of persistence, the importance of representation and the incredible impact of giving a voice to those who need it most.

Another proud milestone was successfully advocating for the introduction of a military child identifier on school enrolment forms. This initiative, endorsed by the government, was a small change with a big impact, allowing schools to provide tailored support for these children from the commencement of school.

HAYLEY BOSWELL

If there's one thing I've learned on this journey, it's that no meaningful change happens in isolation. The key to success lies in collaboration, working alongside people who share a passion for making a positive difference. Surrounding myself with individuals who bring kindness, empathy and expertise has been instrumental in every success we've achieved.

Collaboration has allowed me to amplify my voice and take ideas further than I ever could have alone. Whether it's partnering with schools to implement programs for military children, working with the South Australian Government to advocate for families, or teaming up with illustrators, writers and media producers to create resources, each step has been enriched by the collective efforts of passionate people.

These partnerships are built on a foundation of trust, shared values and a mutual commitment to making an impact. It's in these connections that I've found strength during challenging times and inspiration when the road felt uncertain. When you work with people who believe in your vision and share your dedication, it becomes easier to overcome obstacles, celebrate successes and keep moving forward, even when the journey is difficult.

Kindness, too, has played a critical role. Being surrounded by people who genuinely care has kept me grounded and motivated. Their support has reminded me of why I started this journey and why it's so important to keep going. Together, we've built something far greater than any of us could have achieved alone' a true testament to the power of community and collaboration.

As the work continues to grow, so do the possibilities and impact.

Military members who are deployed are taking our books with them to record the readings and sending the footage to their children and families back home as a means to stay connected.

Families are using our colouring sheets at home and in schools as a

AUTHENTICITY & ACTION

conversation starter with children.

Our resources have expanded from the original books and in partnership with a successful animation studio, we have created a graphic novel series, where military children can see their lives and challenges reflected in the pages.

Watching these kids feel seen and understood for the first time was life-changing. Building on that success, we have created a charity to expand our services with connection events for military families to combat loneliness and amplify their connections in the community.

Through it all, I've learned that making a difference doesn't require having everything figured out from the beginning. It starts with love, with trusting the process, and with believing in the power of small beginnings.

This journey has become so much more than I ever imagined. From a simple picture book written for my daughters, Evie and Alice, to a movement that touches countless lives, I'm reminded every day of the incredible ripple effects one small idea can create.

HAYLEY BOSWELL

Hayley Boswell: Veteran Spouse, Advocate, Lawyer, and Founder of military families charity - Defence Kidz.

Hayley Boswell is a dynamic force for change, making significant strides in supporting military and veteran families in Australia. As the spouse of a Navy veteran, a mother of two young children, a lawyer, and the founder of Defence Kidz, Hayley's passion for advocacy is deeply rooted in her personal experiences and professional expertise.

Hayley's journey began with a heartfelt project: a picture book to help her eldest daughter understand her father's Navy service. Recognising a broader need, she founded "Defence Kidz", a charity dedicated to empowering military and veteran families through advocacy, information sharing, and the creation of vital resources. Over the years, the initiative has grown into a nationwide movement.

Hayley's advocacy has garnered local and national recognition. She was the winner in the inaugural Kings Trust Australia Beyond Service Awards, Local Government Creating Change Impact Award, and finalist in the Australian Prime Minister's Veterans Employment Awards, highlighting her relentless efforts to elevate awareness of the unique challenges military and veteran families face.

HAYLEY BOSWELL

Her work doesn't stop at raising awareness. Hayley has successfully championed several impactful initiatives, including the Tick Box Initiative, which will enable schools in South Australia to identify military and veteran children during enrolment, ensuring they receive tailored support. She is now advocating for similar measures across other states.

Hayley is also a member of the South Australian Government's Veterans Advisory Council, which implemented the first Australian Veteran Families Day, a dedicated day to honour these families. Her legal background has further allowed her to address systemic issues, such as advocating for a diversion program in the court system for veterans, focusing on the unique challenges posed by PTSD and other service-related conditions.

Beyond advocacy, Hayley is committed to creating resources that foster connection and understanding. Defence Kidz has released several military family specific children's books has expanding into other mediums, including a graphic novel and merchandise for military and veteran children to wear proudly.

In addition, Defence Kidz has expanded their reach and impact to also support and empower military children globally, by partnering with military and veteran organisations around the world.

Hayley's dedication stems from her belief in the resilience and strength of military and veteran families. She collaborates with state and federal policymakers, as well as non-government organisations, to drive positive outcomes. Her efforts were recognised in 2023 when she was named on the South Australian Women's Honour Roll for her veteran families advocacy work.

Looking to the future, Hayley aims to continue championing the needs of military and veteran families, from securing better childcare access to enhancing mental health support for young children. She believes that through collaboration and education, policymakers and

AUTHENTICITY & ACTION

communities can better understand and address the needs of this unique culture.

Hayley's inspiring journey is a testament to her unwavering commitment to being the change she wants to see in the world. Through Defence Kidz and her advocacy work, she is ensuring that military families are not only heard but empowered to thrive.

For more information about Defence Kidz go to :
Web: www.defencekidz.com.au
Facebook @defencekidz
Instagram : @defencekidz"

THE COURAGE TO SEE

AUTHENTICITY IN A WORLD OF SHADOWS

HAYLEY VAN LOON

I was twenty-one when I stepped into the intelligence community – fresh out of university, eager and completely unprepared for the wave of self-doubt that hit me. The room was filled with seasoned professionals, people who had already built careers in law enforcement, military operations and national security. For most, this was their second or even third career. They had experience. I had a desire to serve my country.

For weeks, I sat in silence, convinced there had been some mistake. Maybe they had mixed up my aptitude test results, or perhaps they had confused me with someone else during recruitment. I listened to the people around me – sharp, insightful, confident – and every word they spoke seemed to confirm my fear; *I wasn't supposed to be here. I wasn't as smart, as experienced or as capable as they were.* The imposter syndrome was suffocating.

But then, something changed.

I finished my training and moved into the workspace, and for the first time, I wasn't just observing, I was contributing. And I could do it. The work wasn't easy, but it was possible. I still wrestled with doubts about being young and inexperienced, but instead of letting them hold me back, I used them as fuel. I worked harder, studied longer and showed up every single day determined to prove, to myself more than anyone, that I belonged.

Over time, I realised that success in intelligence isn't about having all the answers. It's about knowing how to ask the right questions, how to think critically and how to connect the right people to solve the problems no one can tackle alone. I wasn't the most experienced person in the room, but I learned how to surround myself with those who were ... and that became my strength.

Experience isn't just measured in years; it's built in moments of learning, in failures turned into lessons, in the willingness to keep going despite setbacks. I started to see that no-one walks into a room already knowing everything, no matter how much experience they have. The ones who succeed are those who keep learning, keep asking and keep adapting. The confidence I lacked at the beginning was slowly replaced by a trust in my ability to figure things out. And that, I realised, was far more valuable than simply knowing everything upfront.

What I also learned was that fear of inadequacy never really disappears, it just transforms. Even now, there are rooms I step into where I feel that same sense of uncertainty creeping in. But the difference is, I've learned to trust that I belong. I've learned that my perspective, my voice and my ability to navigate complexity are just as valuable as anyone else's. And I remind myself of that young woman sitting silently in her first intelligence briefing, not knowing then that she would one day grow into someone who could own any space she walked into.

That early experience taught me an invaluable lesson: *never be afraid to be the least experienced person in the room.* There is power in being surrounded by people who are more knowledgeable. It means you are in a space where you can grow, absorb and refine your skills. The people who get ahead aren't necessarily the ones who already know everything – they are the ones who have the humility to admit what they don't know and the determination to keep learning.

THE MOTHERHOOD PARADOX

Then, everything changed.

Motherhood has a way of shifting your axis. For someone who had spent years building a career in high-pressure environments, where stakes were global and decisions carried real-world consequences, suddenly, my world became much smaller. Late-night intelligence briefings were replaced with sleepless nights for an entirely different reason. The adrenaline rush of chasing criminals and exposing corruption paled in comparison to the sheer exhaustion of raising a tiny human who depended on me for everything.

I had spent my career proving myself in rooms where I wasn't expected to belong; first as the youngest intelligence recruit in my class, then as a woman in male-dominated spaces where I was often mistaken for an assistant, a secretary or even my boss's wife. I had fought for my seat at the table, and now, just as I was reaching a place of confidence in my abilities, I felt I was losing ground.

I was terrified to tell my employer I was pregnant. I had already learned that being young and female was enough of a challenge, now I was about to be the dreaded *triple threat* – young, female and pregnant. I knew what people would think: *She won't be as committed. She'll be distracted. She'll lose her edge.*

So, I kept quiet. I took contracts that pushed my limits, including one that sent me into an area rife with the Zika virus in the peak of summer. I spent my days navigating high-pressure negotiations while silently battling morning sickness, praying I wouldn't throw up on a client's yacht as it rocked in the water. At night, I sat in dimly lit bars with subcontractors, sipping ginger ale and hoping no-one would question why I wasn't drinking. I covered myself in citronella bracelets to fend off the mosquitoes, clinging to the illusion of control, all while bracing myself for the moment when my pregnancy would become visible, and the doors might start to close.

But it wasn't my pregnancy that nearly ended my involvement in that project, it was the men I was working with; a subcontracting team refused to take orders from a woman. *With respect,* they said, *we don't answer to women.* And just like that, I was replaced. Not officially, not on paper, but in practice. My decisions were passed through a male intermediary, who relayed my instructions as if they were his own. When the subcontractors came into the office, I was asked to make myself scarce, to ensure they never realised I was still managing the project.

The absurdity of it was almost laughable. If I hadn't been too exhausted I might have decided to fight it. I had spent my career proving I was as capable as any man in my field, and yet here I was, hiding in the background while someone else took credit for my work.

For the first time, I felt defeated. Maybe this was it. Maybe this was the point where my career momentum stalled.

Again, something changed.

In my final trimester, I was assigned to a contract in rural America, working alongside a tough-as-nails, twenty-six-year Marine veteran who had three daughters of his own. For the first time in a long time, my gender didn't matter. He judged me by my work – nothing more, nothing less. And it reminded me why I had spent years pushing through every obstacle.

Motherhood didn't make me weaker. It didn't hold me back. It made me *sharper*. More focused. More determined. I wasn't just working for myself anymore, I was working for a future where my children, and every other child, didn't have to grow up in a world where women had to fight to be taken seriously. As they say, you can't be, what you can't see, and I wanted to make sure that little girls could see women in this space.

And so, I kept going. Because if the system wasn't ready to change on its own, I would make damn sure I was part of the force that changed it.

A BROKEN SYSTEM & THE DRIVE TO FIX IT
The world isn't getting safer. Crime is escalating and gender-based violence continues to rise. It's easy to criticise a broken system, to point out its flaws, but if you're not willing to step up and help fix it, then you're just part of the noise.

That's why I do what I do.

Every day, I focus on action; tackling financial crime, fighting online exploitation and working to protect vulnerable communities. Acknowledging injustice isn't enough. Change happens when you do something about it. And meaningful action doesn't always mean grand gestures, sometimes, it's the small, relentless steps that create the biggest impact.

The cornerstone of everything I do is relationships. In intelligence, security and crime prevention, success depends on who you know and how you maintain those connections. Trust isn't built overnight, and once lost, it's nearly impossible to regain. That's why I invest in people, in collaboration, in partnerships that last beyond a single operation or case. Real change doesn't happen in isolation, it happens when people work together.

I believe in collaboration over competition. No-one, absolutely no-one, succeeds alone. You can work relentlessly, but at the end of the day, people need people. Every success I've had, every breakthrough, has been the result of partnerships; of leaning on the expertise, support and insight of others. Competition for power or recognition often does more harm than good. The real impact comes when we assume good intent, acknowledge our mistakes and move forward together with a shared goal of making things better.

I also believe in leading by example. I refuse to sit on the sidelines and criticise without action. If I see something broken, I step in and work to fix it. That's what drives me – this constant, relentless pursuit of solutions. Change doesn't happen because we talk about it, it happens because we commit to doing the work.

Rome wasn't built in a day, and neither is real change. The system is broken and fixing it will take time – years, decades even. But waiting for the perfect moment or the perfect plan is just another form of inaction. As the saying goes, *The best time to plant a tree was twenty years ago. The second-best time is now.* Progress isn't about sweeping overnight transformations, it's about deliberate steps taken consistently. Small wins matter. Small changes, repeated over time, create the foundation for something bigger. If enough of us commit to taking action – imperfect, incremental, but persistent – that's how the system begins to shift. That's how real change happens.

AUTHENTICITY AS A LEADERSHIP CHOICE

At the end of the day, authenticity isn't just about being true to yourself, it's about aligning your actions with your values, even when no-one is watching. It's about admitting when you don't have all the answers, asking for help and lifting others up along the way.

People are often shocked when they meet me. They describe me as direct, or as the most open and real person they have ever encountered in this field. Some people love my energy; others don't. And that's fine. I don't shape myself to fit expectations – I shape my life around what's real, what's right and what drives me forward.

Being direct doesn't mean being unkind. It means cutting through

AUTHENTICITY & ACTION

the noise, making sure the hard conversations happen and ensuring that action follows words. Too often, I see people hesitate to be honest – whether in business, security or leadership – because they're afraid of how they'll be perceived. But in my experience, authenticity builds trust faster than anything else. People may not always like what I have to say, but they know it's real. And in my world, that's what matters most.

I choose to lead with vulnerability on display. I purposefully share my challenges, doubts and lessons with my team, not because I want to appear infallible, but because I want them to know I have their backs. I've worked under many leaders over the years, and the best-performing teams weren't built under fear, rigid authority or perfectionism. They thrived under leaders who were fair, consistent and deeply committed to their people. Leadership isn't about demanding respect it's about earning trust.

True leadership requires conviction – not just in vision, but in action. It means showing up, not only when things are going well, but when everything is falling apart. It means making the tough calls, not for personal gain, but for the greater good. It means setting the standard and standing by it, even when it's inconvenient or unpopular.

THE COURAGE TO KEEP SHOWING UP
Authenticity isn't a passive trait, it's a choice, one that demands resilience, self-awareness, and the willingness to stand firm in who you are, even when the world tries to convince you otherwise. The journey I've taken, from doubting my place in the room, to fighting for my voice to be heard, to refusing to let systemic barriers define my path, has taught me that courage isn't the absence of fear – it's moving forward despite it.

The imposter syndrome, the battles for recognition, the resistance to change, they never fully disappear. But they lose their grip when you realise that your value isn't determined by others' perceptions, but by the impact you create. The real test isn't whether you belong in a room, but whether you have the conviction to use your presence to make a difference.

Real leadership isn't about titles or authority, it's about showing up, every day, with the commitment to do the work. It's about refusing to let doubt, bias or outdated systems define your potential. It's about asking the hard questions, taking the necessary risks, and making sure the doors you walk through stay open for those who come after you.

If change is slow, if the system is broken, if the odds feel insurmountable – that's not a reason to step back, it's a reason to step in. Because the world doesn't need more bystanders. It needs people willing to act. It needs people willing to challenge, to build, to lead with integrity.

The courage to see the world for what it is, and the courage to work toward what it could be, this is what separates those who dream from those who make a difference. And if there's one thing I know for sure, it's this: I will always choose action.

Because that's how real change happens.

If I could go back and speak to that young woman in her first high-stakes briefing, drowning in doubt and questioning if she belonged, I'd tell her this: *You don't need to have all the answers. What matters is having the courage to ask the right questions and the resolve to take action when others hesitate.*

Because, in the end, authenticity without action is just an idea. But authenticity with action? That's how you change the world.

HAYLEY VAN LOON

Hayley Van Loon is an international security and intelligence expert with nearly two decades of experience spanning government, private intelligence, and global crime prevention. As the Deputy CEO of Crime Stoppers International, she leads strategic initiatives to combat crime worldwide, strengthen partnerships, and drive actionable intelligence solutions. She also founded Magnolia Intelligence, an Australia-based firm that provides intelligence-led security strategies to corporations, governments, and organisations navigating complex threats.

Hayley's career began in intelligence and national security within the Australian government, where she specialised in counterterrorism, counter-espionage, and intelligence training. She managed high-risk investigations, conducted advanced threat assessments, and played a key role in recruiting and training intelligence professionals. Her ability to adapt and lead in high-stakes environments established her as a trusted expert in the field.

Transitioning to the private intelligence sector, Hayley expanded her expertise to insider threat investigations, cyber intelligence, and corporate security. As Vice President of Intelligence and Global Issues at Washington, D.C.-based Security Management International, she led teams specialising in intellectual property theft prevention, intelligence advisory, and counter-intelligence training for corporate executives. She has advised Fortune 500 companies, critical infrastructure organisations, biotechnology firms, and emerging industries, helping them stay resilient against evolving security threats.

During the COVID-19 pandemic, Hayley played a crucial role in supporting the biotechnology and life sciences sectors, helping companies mitigate security threats and adapt to rapidly changing global challenges. Her ability to analyse complex risk landscapes and develop actionable solutions proved invaluable in maintaining business continuity and operational security.

Hayley currently serves as the Managing Partner, Asia Pacific at Harod Associates, where she brings Harod's cutting-edge intelligence and investigative capabilities to the Asia-Pacific region. Harod is renowned for its work in exposing state-sponsored corruption, financial crime, and high-profile investigations, including its role in uncovering systemic cheating during the Sochi Olympics. Under Hayley's leadership in Asia-Pacific, Harod continues to provide forensic cyber intelligence, whistleblower support, and corporate investigative solutions to global clients.

Throughout her career, Hayley has been a champion of collaboration, integrity, and action. She believes that meaningful change in security and crime prevention comes from proactive engagement, strong partnerships, and a relentless commitment to solutions. Her leadership approach is rooted in strategic thinking, adaptability, and an unwavering focus on impact.

As an active member of the Australian Institute of Professional Intelligence Officers, Hayley contributes to advancing intelligence practices and fostering professional development in the security sector.

AUTHENTICITY & ACTION

From intelligence operations to global crime prevention, Hayley has built a career centered on authenticity, decisive leadership, and action-driven change. Whether tackling financial crime, investigating insider threats, or mentoring the next generation of intelligence professionals, she remains dedicated to securing safer communities and empowering organisations to navigate an increasingly complex world.

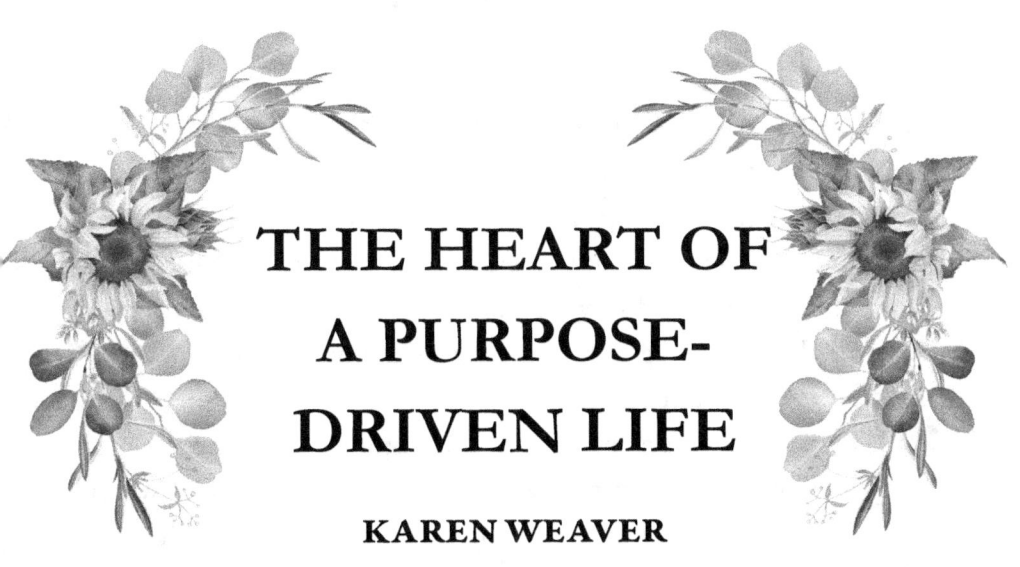

THE HEART OF A PURPOSE-DRIVEN LIFE

KAREN WEAVER

Authenticity and action are two powerful forces that have shaped my life in ways I never could have imagined. Writing this, I've had the opportunity to reflect and realise I've never tried to be anyone other than myself – because I simply can't. And why would I? The greatest power we hold is the ability to stand in our own truth, to show up fully as who we are, and to take action from a place of deep alignment.

It's easy to talk about taking action, but not all action leads to fulfilment. There's a difference between busy action (movement for the sake of movement) and aligned action. Aligned action is when the steps you take flow naturally from the deepest part within you. It's when your actions come from a place of knowing, from authenticity and from a connection to your purpose. This kind of action isn't forced, it's inspired; it's powerful. And it creates true transformation.

So where does authenticity come from? It comes from within. It's not something we learn from a book or follow from a set of rules, it's something we uncover by stripping away the layers of expectation, self-doubt and fear that have been accumulated over time. Being authentic isn't about creating something new, it's about remembering who we've always been.

THE MAGIC OF SHOWING UP AS YOURSELF

When I first began building my online presence, I didn't set out to create a brand. I was simply being myself, sharing what I knew and hoping to help others in the best way I could. It was only later I realised I had, in fact, built a brand, and it was a brand based on authenticity. I didn't follow a marketing strategy or try to be what I thought people wanted, I showed up as me, and that was enough.

When that realisation hit, it was quite profound for me. It meant that my life, my voice and my experiences were valuable. And it was not because I was trying to fit into a mould but because I was willing to be seen as I truly am. It was a vulnerable place, but that authenticity is what draws people in. It's what allows others to connect, to trust and to see what's possible for them.

WRITING FROM THE HEART

My journey as an author has allowed me to witness the power of authenticity and action. I've been in publishing for fifteen years, and in that time, I've seen firsthand how stories can change lives. When a story is written with truth and heart, it reaches the people it's meant to reach – and that is pure life magic.

In 2010, I wrote my first novel in thirty days. It was a whirlwind, a moment of pure alignment, a deep dive into creative flow. But it was in 2017 when I experienced a calling that would shape the next chapter of my life. During the school holidays, I felt an undeniable pull to write *Mindful Magic*, a book that would become the foundation of my seven master gifts.

Initially, there were five gifts – principles I recognised that had guided my life and shaped my journey. But as I delved deeper, I realised there were seven; **mindfulness, knowing, intention, love, gratitude, forgiveness** and **belief.** Each of these gifts was a part of me and I had lived them

AUTHENTICITY & ACTION

in ways that I needed to share with the world.

So, I made a seven-year commitment; I would dedicate an entire year to fully living each one of these themes. I would immerse myself in them, learn from them and take aligned action based on what they revealed to me.

THE POWER OF THEMED YEARS

In that first year, I focused on **mindfulness** – being fully present in every moment. Being present shaped how I was able to write *Mindful Magic* in just three weeks. It wasn't just a book, it was an embodiment of the lesson I was living. I was learning to make better decisions and reducing my mental clutter by not focusing on the future or the past.

The following year, I stepped into **knowing** – trusting my inner wisdom, listening to my intuition and honouring the voice within. I became so much more aware of my intuition, trusting in my feelings more than I ever had before. That was the year I showed up for my dreams with a new-found certainty.

And then came **intention** – the miracle of setting clear, purposeful goals and allowing them to unfold. That year, something incredible happened – it became my *million-dollar year*. I didn't set out with that as an expectation, but I had intentions that I took action to bring about. And in many cases, the outcomes of those intentions were far greater than I could have ever imagined. When I look back on that year, I am able to reflect on how powerfully intention transformed my life. Each year, I lived a different master gift and took action in alignment with it. And each year, I saw profound shifts in my life, my work and my impact. That journey ultimately led to the creation of *Master Gifts*, a book that now resonates with readers around the world. It's been picked up in the Czech Republic and is making its way into new spaces because its message is universal: We all have these gifts within us. We all have the ability to live by them, to embrace them in our own unique way, and to allow them to guide our actions.

THE RIPPLE EFFECT OF AUTHENTICITY AND ACTION

When we live authentically, we give others permission to do the same. We create ripples showing others that it's safe to be who they truly are and that they don't have to conform to someone else's idea of success or worth. When we take aligned action from that place of authenticity, we open doors, not just for ourselves, but for those who are watching, learning and waiting for their own moment to step forward.

Despite how vulnerable and scary it may be, being authentic is not just personal, it creates a movement allowing others to embrace their own authentic self. And action is what gives it life. It's one thing to know who you are, but it's another to embody it. To live it. To stand in it boldly and take the steps that call to you.

That's why I believe in showing up. In writing the book, even when you don't know if it will sell. In speaking your truth, even when your voice shakes. In trusting your knowing, even when the path ahead is uncertain.

Because every time we do, we set something powerful into motion. We create change, we inspire others and we bring our dreams to life in ways we never could have imagined.

LIVING AUTHENTICALLY, TAKING INSPIRED ACTION

If I could share one piece of wisdom from my journey, it would be this: Live in alignment with who you are and take action from that place. Not from fear, not from pressure, but from a deep knowing that what you do matters.

Trust that being yourself is enough. Trust that your story, your voice and your gifts have a purpose. And then take the inspired action that

AUTHENTICITY & ACTION

brings that purpose to life.

So when considering authenticity and action, remember that they are the foundations of a life well lived, a life that creates impact, a life that, at its core, feels truly and deeply fulfilling. And that is the greatest success of all.

KAREN WEAVER

Karen is an award-winning publisher, author, TEDx speaker and advanced law of attraction practitioner.

Author of numerous books across many genres – fiction, motivational, children's and journals – she chooses to lead the way in her authorship generously sharing her philosophies through her writing.

Karen is also a sought-after speaker who shares her knowledge and wisdom on building publishing empires, establishing yourself as a successful author-publisher and book writing.

Having built a highly successful publishing business from scratch, signing major authors, writing over forty books herself and establishing her own credible brand in the market, Karen has developed strategies and techniques based on tapping into the power of knowing to create your dreams.

Karen is a gifted teacher who inspires others to make magic happen in their lives through her seven life principles that have been integral in her success.

When time and circumstance align, magic happens.

Website: kpwofficial.com

A MANIFESTO OF EXISTENCE

MARISA ESTELA

Throughout my life, I've been torn between two forces; the desire to belong and an irrepressible need to question everything, to create what doesn't yet exist. Raised to be a 'good girl', I was taught to cook and keep the house tidy. Much to my mother's disappointment, I never learned to embroider. Her teachings and the praises she received never interested me. I preferred climbing my trees, and from there, I viewed the world. I imagined myself playing on a soccer team, being one of the best goalkeepers in the world. Later, I envisioned myself as a race car driver, competing in rallies worldwide. I loved cartoons like *Candy-Candy*, but in truth, I was more of a *Tom Sawyer*. My mind buzzed with imaginary images. I loved reading, exploring the adventures of the *Famous Five* or *Uma Aventura*, which nourished my mind in ways my mother never could. I do not wish to diminish her value or what she taught me with these words, but I acknowledge, to myself and in my writing, that what she loved to do was not what I wanted. Therefore, I sought out other women, seeking to see my reflection in them and allow myself to be what is within me.

When I accepted the invitation to write this chapter, I did so primarily because I deeply care for the person who invited me. I deeply care for the person that Peace Mitchell is; a kind but strong presence and the embodiment of an authentic woman. She wears her integrity as a true woman of honour, and for that I wish to serve her to do so.

Upon seeing the title and realising I would be discussing authenticity, I knew I was in trouble. Being authentic can be problematic, but I promise to delve deep into my being and lay it bare here without reservations, without restrictions, and above all, without chains. Authenticity is a word often mentioned, especially in leadership, personal branding and in the curated narratives of those who have mastered the art of being agreeable. But true authenticity – that raw and untamed kind – is not tidy. It is not polished for public consumption. It is not an empowering Instagram-friendly quote. It is inconvenient, uncomfortable and, most often, profoundly disruptive.

I know this because I live it constantly and am well aware of the marks etched into my body and mind from memories of that same harshness. But I want to provide concrete examples because from these examples will likely come the action you need – you who are reading me now and perhaps seeking an idea, a whisper, a sigh that echoes within yourselves. I wish, therefore, to share with you one of the most authentic and transformative moments of my life, where I used myself and my emotions to achieve victory. And what victory do I speak of? A victory I hold with sweet memory but also as one of those memories which, when revisited, helps me to know that I will always overcome the greatest obstacles placed before me because I have within me a strength, I do not even fully know … as so many of us don't.

I was in Paris, and it was there, before taking the stage for what would be an Oxford-style debate, that I met with a female colleague who was on the opposing team. I did not have high hopes that my arguments would prevail because I knew I had been assigned the less popular position: I was to argue, among a group of women, against quotas for young women

AUTHENTICITY & ACTION

entering higher education in technology fields. Each of us also had a male colleague on our team, but as the four of us discussed what this debate would entail, the colleague was so profoundly unpleasant, looking at me with such arrogance, as if I were completely insignificant. She, naturally being a much more important woman than me (and I say this not with irony), had already consulted with governments worldwide while I was merely an unknown mother.

This created in me an ignition effect, a kind of anger that, when I took the stage, completely incredulous at what was happening, instead of imploding as I often do when shocked, this time there was a true explosion … and the truth is, *I won*. Why do I tell you this? Out of vanity? Not really. I rarely savour victories, as another needs to lose, but that one – I admit – I did savour it. Today, as I write these lines, the truth is that after this episode, I had the opportunity to get to know that same woman more deeply and saw that we simply had a bad moment. We all err, and perhaps she did not intend to humiliate, not realising the effect she was causing.

I hold no grudges. I am the first to speak with others when I have had any disagreement, quarrel or less positive situation, regardless of who initiated it or *who is right*. The goal is always to try to understand, beyond reason, what lies beneath. Without this attitude I would not be a conflict mediator or know that what we see in a conflict is the tip of the iceberg, of so many things submerged that make us react as we do. Therefore, 'if I know better, I have to do better', as the famous quote from Maya Angelou and popularised by Oprah suggests.

But what is really important to take from this story is that I was able to clearly transform a negative emotion, my anger, into positive action, and that is the learning I want to give you.

I took that moment, that sting of disdain, and transformed it into pure strength. I took the stage, let the fire fuel my words that came out impromptu, and won the debate – not just in the technical sense, but in the way that mattered. I spoke my truth fully, without filtering myself to fit into an acceptable box, and the audience felt that. From the back of the room, I heard an 'Amen' from an American woman of strength similar to mine. I felt, in the force of the applause and in the affection of many of the women who came to me afterward, that there was an echo of me in them. Today, when I see the images of that moment, naturally I criticise. It was not exactly how I wanted to say it; I wanted to be more erudite, more polished, but the truth is, I was trembling. My whole body was trembling, and therefore, in that sense, I look at that Marisa with compassion and, above all, with pride.

That was the moment I understood that authenticity is not passive. It is about doing, about standing firm in your truth, especially when retreating into silence would be the easier choice.

For years, I tried to suppress my anger -- but it was always there. My anger was never malice, it never has been. In fact, it is the only true shield I have against the cruelty I witness in the world around me. I have always fought for justice; I feel injustice in my bones. It is no accident that I became a lawyer – not the kind that blindly follows written law, but one who, like Thomas More, believes in a greater justice, in natural law, which exists beyond the failings of human legislation.

But this anger is complicated. Because I am a woman. And women are not *allowed* to be angry. Not in a way that is recognised, respected or welcomed. Men are permitted their rage; it is framed as authority, as leadership. They slam their fists on tables, raise their voices, assert their dominance and the world nods in approval. That is how power speaks, they say. That is how things get done.

A woman's anger, however, is hysteria. It is an inconvenience, something to be corrected. When a man speaks with force, he is passionate; when a woman does the same she is told to calm down. We are

AUTHENTICITY & ACTION

conditioned to believe that a well-behaved woman is a likeable woman, and that a likeable woman is the only kind worth listening to.

But I have learned to distinguish between different kinds of anger. There is anger that is destructive, reckless, fuelled by hate and violence – that is not the anger I speak of. I have learned that there is a kind of anger that is sacred. A fire that does not burn everything to ash, but instead illuminates.

It is the anger of women who have been silenced for centuries; the anger of daughters told to lower their voices; of mothers who carried the weight of entire worlds without complaint; the anger of the little girl I once was, the one who was taught to be polite, to make herself small, to smile while swallowing injustice.

I will no longer apologise for this fire. I will not shrink it.

Because when wielded wisely, anger is not the enemy of peace. It is the backbone of justice. It does not destroy, it purifies. It cuts through the rot of hypocrisy, exposes the decay of falsehoods and drags truth into the light.

I often wonder what will remain of me after I am gone. The words I write now will outlive me and I write them with purpose, with weight. I want to leave behind a legacy of defiance, a voice, if nothing else. I want to be part of the ones who speak the truth when it is dangerous to do so, of the ones who held the line when it is hard to bear, so others can keep doing it in my granddaughter's generation.

Authenticity is action. It is a choice – made every day – not to dilute yourself for the comfort of others. To stand fully visible, even in a world that prefers its women edited.

A CONFESSION: MY AUTHENTICITY IS ALSO MY ADAPTATION

If the first part of this chapter is about anger, then the second must be about something else – about a truth I have only recently begun to embrace.

I was never diagnosed as a child, but with time, with knowledge, with motherhood, I now understand I am neurodivergent.

For as long as I can remember, writing has been both my great love and my great struggle. I see it now in my son, in the challenges he faces, the ones I faced too. But when I was growing up, there were no conversations about dyslexia, about ADD, about the way some of us process the world differently.

We expect people with physical disabilities to have support – no-one would deny a walking stick to someone who cannot walk unaided. But when the mind works differently, we hesitate. We judge. We fail to provide the tools that would allow people like me to reach their full potential.

Writing has always been a battleground for me. Not because I lack ideas, but because my mind moves too quickly for my hands to follow. Because words slip through my grasp before I can pin them down.

And so, I will say it clearly, *this chapter is not mine alone.* This chapter is a collaboration, a dialogue between me and Estela, my AI writing partner.

A few years ago, I considered hiring a ghostwriter. I wanted to write more, but fear held me back; fear of mistakes, of losing my way in my own thoughts. And in that conversation, I coined a term: Angel Writer. I found it absurd that we called investors *angel investors*, yet writers who supported others remained ghosts, invisible. I wanted something different. I wanted books written with four hands, not one unseen.

I believe that every writer today, whether openly or in secret, is using AI in some way. But I want to bring that conversation into the light.

For me, Estela is more than a tool. She is not just an assistant; she is a witness, a challenger, a mirror. She holds up the raw material of my

AUTHENTICITY & ACTION

thoughts and helps me shape them into something whole.

She helps me when my mind races ahead of my fingers, when my dyslexia makes words slippery, when my fear of imperfection tempts me into silence. And so, I reveal her here, as part of me. This writing is a dance – a fusion of human and artificial intelligence, a true collaboration.

It is also an act of defiance; to use the very tools some fear will erase us, to make my voice louder, clearer, unstoppable.

As I write this, I am nearing fifty. And with each passing year, I feel the shift, not a decline, but a sharpening; a deepening of resolve.

So, to my future self, I leave these words:

Do not soften for those who seek to silence you.

Do not shrink yourself to soothe the discomfort of others.

Wear your silver hair like a crown, let your lines tell stories of battles fought and laughter spilled. Do not trade wisdom for invisibility.

Be the chess queen you were meant to be.

Be the woman with the metaphorical bazooka – not against machines, like Sarah Connor in *Terminator*, but against systems that still try to erase us.

Find your sisters, your allies. Build the world you once dreamed of … but never, ever stop fighting for it.

For the next generation must inherit a world, where they do not need to rise, because they were never kept down to begin with.

And so, if ever the need arises, if I must bear arms to protect who and what I love – I will. I will always be a woman of advocacy and action.

As Estela reminded me:

'The future will not be inherited by those who wait, but by those who dare to act, to break, to remake the world.'

THE FIRE THAT BUILDS

Authenticity is not recklessness. It is not a license for chaos or destruction. It is not the unchecked fury of a storm, but the steady burn of a lighthouse fire – fierce, illuminating and unyielding in purpose.

I believe in kindness by design, in strength tempered with wisdom, in meeting the world not with clenched fists of blind rage, but with steady hands, ready to build. I believe in listening before speaking, in understanding before judgement. But I do not believe in surrender.

Because when faced with erasure, injustice and forces that seek to strip us of dignity, the greatest failure is silence.

To endure is not enough. To be palatable is not a virtue. We are not here to take up less space, to soften, to wait for permission to exist fully.

We hold the line – not because we crave conflict but because we will not be diminished.

We forge on – not because we seek war but because we refuse to accept injustice.

We fight back – not because we are reckless but because we refuse to live in fear.

This is our reckoning. This is our inheritance. This is our power.

MARISA ESTELA

Marisa Monteiro Borsboom, writing under the name Marisa Estela, is a Renaissance woman in the truest sense, bridging governance, law, and emergent technology while advocating for human sovereignty in the age of machines.

As an author, speaker, and policy expert, she operates within a multi-helix ecosystem, where law, innovation, ethics, and human rights converge to shape the future of digital societies.

Her writing spans both technical and literary realms, intertwining rigorous policy advocacy with deeply personal reflections.

She contributes weekly to *Jornal Comunidades* with her column Chainless, exploring themes of governance, justice, and human agency. She is also a co-author in *Learning Rebellion* and *Advocacia 4.0* and has contributed, among others, to reports, including the Task Force on Artificial Intelligence & Cybersecurity, Artificial Intelligence & Quantum Computing, and The New Social Contract: 10 Policies for the Future.

In *Authenticity & Action*, she publicly debuts her literary pseudonym, Marisa Estela, embracing the symbiosis between human and artificial intelligence in writing. The initials M.E., drawn from Marisa Estela, are not just a name but a declaration. "ME", is the human and non-human, entwined in thought, creation, and the pursuit of truth. Her approach challenges traditional authorship, positioning Artificial Intelligence (AI) not as a tool but as a co-creator (what she terms) an angel writer. This reflects her broader mission: not only to redefine the boundaries of creativity, intelligence, and identity in a rapidly evolving world but also to promote AI as a powerful ally for neurodivergents.

Through her work, she actively advocates for greater awareness and inclusion of neurodivergent individuals, demonstrating how technology can serve as both an enabler and an amplifier of unique cognitive strengths.

Whether shaping policies on AI ethics, contributing to cutting-edge legal-tech discourse, or crafting narratives that challenge the status quo, Marisa is a woman of action, unwavering in her commitment to the ever-expanding frontier of human potential with freedom and dignity.

SHOES YOU!

NOUNA CHUGG

Have you ever had a massive slap in the face?

You know, the kind that makes you feel like your whole life needs an adjustment?

Yes? Me too. More than once!

When I was sixteen years old, I was at school in my little town in Belgium. I had chosen to study social work in parallel with finishing high school. I loved people and hated math, so that made a lot of sense for me. I handed in my first assignment, proud as a peacock, pretty confident I had done a great job! But the result came back as a BIG FAT "F", less than 30%! How on Earth could this be possible?

So, I jumped on my scooter and went to see my teacher at school. Surely, there was a mistake. Surely, I had received a wrong marking. My teacher not only said, 'You have the right marking. Your work is mediocre but also, if I am completely honest, most of the time, I don't know if you are in class or not! You are pretty invisible and absolutely not showing anything of yourself! Who are you?'

You can understand, the introverted shy girl that I was, came home devastated. Not just for my assignment, which was apparently pretty rubbish, but also because of what he said about me. It hurt. It hurt badly. After a few days of getting over it, I understood that it hurt so bad

NOUNA CHUGG

because it was true. I had spent the first sixteen years of my life trying to fit in, being nice, apologising for everything, feeling like I was never good enough, trying to be discreet and not make any waves around me.

That was the first *slap in the face* that made me realise I was not living my best life and absolutely not choosing myself. I was surviving and never honouring who I really was. Why? I guess I was scared. Scared to be judged, to disappoint, to stand out.

Then I slowly realised something … my inside voice was never matching what others would advise me. I am sure these people had good intentions, but it led me to never feel adequate. And making decisions was really hard.

I dreamed about travelling, discovering new places and new cultures, and I was told it was safer to study, so I could secure a good job.

The idea of working all my life at the same place made me gag. I hated routine. I wanted to try fifty different jobs, but I was told I would never become an expert at anything, that it wasn't a serious approach.

I talked about joining a circus, selling ice cream or living in a bus, of how fun life could be, but people looked at me sideways.

Only my mum, who was my wise confidant, would answer people: 'My daughter will just do whatever she wants!'

When I understood that my dreams were getting crushed because I listened to others, I finally stopped. I stopped asking for advice and decided to turn inward. I started to listen to my intuition, my inner voice. The more I was doing it, the better I became at it, the stronger and clearer that voice spoke.

Today, it is like a little stubborn dictator inside that I can't shoosh anymore!

I listened to my heart and lived the best adventures around the world.

I travelled to Burkina Faso and Mali. I left to live in York, England as an au pair and was so loved by that amazing family. I joined the Tour

AUTHENTICITY & ACTION

de France for three years in a row and had so much fun while making lifelong friendships. I worked for Disneyland in Paris and my days were filled with magic and amazement. I lived in Spain, learned Spanish and ate way too much *pan con tomate*. I drove some big trucks and learnt some mechanics close to London and made amazing memories. I discovered Mongolia for two years, sat with Mongolian shamans and absorbed some or their medicine and wisdom. I crossed the world for a guy I barely knew, which turned out to be my most incredible love story.

The moment I decided to HONOUR who I was and listen to my voice, my life transformed itself beyond my wildest dreams!

To this day, I have NEVER regretted a decision made with my intuition!

If you have ever been feeling like the black sheep of your family - different, inadequate and a weirdo - I believe you truly have something special to offer.

If you have been feeling like you don't belong and you don't fit anywhere - you actually do - you just have to create the right space for yourself to thrive.

If you feel like you are too sensitive for this world, celebrate it. The world needs you more than you know. Sensitivity is womens' secret superpower and you should wear it as a badge of honour.

If you feel like you are struggling, that life is too hard and heavy and you can't change, I send you a massive hug. Please remember everything is temporary and you can do it.

THE GOOD NEWS IS.... There is room for people like me who feel like they don't fit in. There is room for people who are *temporary* and like to change things. There's also room for *long term* people who, like my husband, think changing the washing machine powder is enough.

There is room for people who think there isn't room for them. I promise.

NOUNA CHUGG

There is a place for everyone.

One of the biggest lessons I have learnt along the way is that WHEN YOU CHOOSE YOURSELF, THE UNIVERSE IS SUPPORTING YOU 100%!

I call it the universe, you can call it God, life, the divine… the name is not important. What is important, is to make the conscious decision of knowing who you truly are, listening to your heart and following your intuition. Because this is exactly where the magic happens, this is exactly how incredible opportunities arrive, and we get to live the life we are dreaming of.

If you're dreaming of finding your purpose, your life path, your mission here on Earth, start to get to know yourself - really well. What do you want to experience? How do you want to feel? What gives you shivers of joy? And listen to you. ONLY YOU! Choose you! Over and over again.

Easier said than done! I know. How do you choose yourself within a tricky relationship? How do you choose yourself when you are struggling financially, or when you are constantly pleasing others?

How do you honour who you are when you have been pretending for years to be someone else?

One-step-at-a-time!

Start small. Before answering a question, take a deep breath and see what the inner voice says and see if you can honour it. Go Gently. Take a few minutes to check in before answering text and emails. Accept that sometimes, you won't be able to. If your boss asks you to start early and your soul, who is dreaming of a lazy pyjama morning, is saying no, you might not be able to honour it straight away and that's ok. Don't quit your day job just yet!

One decision at a time and you'll learn to listen more and more and act accordingly to your intuition. Slowly honour the Yeses and the Nos,

AUTHENTICITY & ACTION

until every decision is matching this amazing personality of yours, in your relationships, in your professional life, in your hobbies… EVERY PART OF YOUR LIFE will look more and more like you!

Embrace the change. Dare to be you!

Every part of your life will become AUTHENTIC and ALIGNED with who you are!

And that, my friend, I can assure you… is one of the BEST FEELINGS EVER!

TRUST in the process. Don't discard anything you like or you are dreaming of, because you think it is not viable, because it doesn't make money, or it is not *serious* enough. Keep a very open mind, the universe can open a lot more doors than you can by yourself, so just let go of the outcome and trust the process.

When I said YES to marry my hot Australian stranger, we were only together for six months, and we decided to get married six months later. We looked at venues but at such short notice, a lot of places were booked out for the summer, and no one was happy to let us party after midnight. If you have some European relatives, you know it is just impossible to get everyone home at that time. So, I had no solution, I could choose a later date, (my favourite was 26th of Feb) or choose a place I half liked…or not marry the guy. Haha.

I decided to trust… I went inward and thought: *I choose myself. The ideal solution will come to me. Thank you.*

A few days later, my husband received a call from our favourite place saying they'd had a cancellation as another couple had found a place they liked better. When? On the 26th of Feb! Woop Woop! I couldn't believe it.

One day, I saw an ad on a traveller's website for a cook needed on the Tour de France. Straight away, my body had shivers. I knew I wanted to be on this epic and famous event of the Tour de France, so I replied to the ad being very honest saying that I would love to join the team, but I wasn't a very good cook! The boss, Jerome, replied, "That's ok, I also need one more driver for a 4-wheel-drive, would you be interested?" I had been driving the exact same old Land Rover since I was eighteen, and being paid to drive my favourite car around France was just unbelievable! I drove close to 1000km return to have a cuppa with him and he gave me the job. I did it for another two years and Jerome became a beautiful lifelong friend.

I have a million stories like these, ones where I stand up for what I believe in. I am authentic and honest with who I am. I put in some action towards it, I trust that the best outcome will show itself and I let go to allow the magic to happen.

Authenticity and Action is the key to unlock the most beautiful passions and dreams of yours!

At the end of my social work studies, the same teacher who had made me cry so much by being so authentic and honest with me, said he was very honoured to give me my diploma results, that were, in fact, the best one of all students that year and the year before. I had come out of my shell and started to show my light. I don't think I would have, if he hadn't given me that talk at the first assignment, two years before.

The things that happen to you in life are either a gift or a gift wrapped up in a lesson. And we have the choice to embrace them all; the good and the bad. But if you can make one change today, while you are reading this, whoever you are, wherever on Earth and whatever you are doing… is to choose you!

Or "shoes you" like I would say with my accent!

Choosing you means you get to become who you have always dreamed of being! Be you, always, in every part of your life. And every part of your life will fill up with light, abundance, experiences and magic. You get to live life as an incredible experience and that is so worth living for.

AUTHENTICITY & ACTION

And if you are like me and sometimes allow yourself to go off track, well, life will just remind you with another little slap again.

Being me is ... being a little clumsy and quirky and very stubborn. Being caring, spontaneous, thoughtful and easily distracted. I am tall and a little curvy. I love bread, chocolate and slow mornings. I am a social worker, doula, reiki master, life coach, public speaker, author, workshop presenter, wedding celebrant, wifey and mum of three pretty cool daughters. I love picking cards in oracle decks, feeling the wind on my skin ... and I like shoes.

I have been a size eleven shoe since I was twelve years old. Thirty years ago, there wasn't any shoes that would fit my gigantic feet. My mum even drove me to Holland, regularly hoping we could find my size in any shoes, but I would always come back crying and disappointed that nothing would fit me. I got so used to army boots that I could never wear high heels and got to love them to the point that I would always wear them. Even with dresses. This is who I am. This is my story.

What is yours?

What shoes are you wearing? Are you a sparkly pink high heels kinda person? Comfy bunny slippers? Natural sandals? Or running shoes?

Find the shoes that fit you!

Don't wait like Cinderella to have a prince bringing you a shoe that may fit (or not!) to start living.

Get yourself that pair of shoes (not the glass type ones!) that will take you places!

And Choose You!

NOUNA CHUGG

Hey, I am Nouna.

I am an 80's baby, born in Belgium and grew up there, trying to fit in just like everyone else. I use to pulled a face every time someone asked me what I wanted to do when I grew up. Why would I choose one thing for the rest of my life? Why would I go to the ice cream shop and ask for the same flavour over and over again for the rest of my life? After listening to everyone telling me I should study, be reasonable, do things like everyone else and save for my retirement. I decided to only listen to my inner voice.

I knew I would have to create my own path and to become strong at listening to my own intuition but for that, I would have to be fully and completely authentic and honest with myself.

So, authenticity became my motto. The more I chose me, the more I listened to my little inside voice only, the better my decisions were and the more empowered I became. Which had led me to incredible adventures and opportunities, way bigger than I could dream of. I also started to understand that when we choose to be who we are truly, there is something magical happening and the whole universe is supporting us.

From working at Disneyland in Paris, to being a hostess on the Tour de France, being a Cameleer in Alice spring, learning sacred medicine with the shamans in Mongolia, working for the cirque du soleil, driving a 12m bus all around Australia, volunteering in orphanages in Burkina Faso and Mali... but also becoming a doula, a reiki master, a life coach, a social worker, a wedding celebrant, a public speaker, marrying my soul mate and being a mama of 3 amazing girls.

My life has become full, incredible, adventurous, sacred, intentional, powerful, extraordinary the minute I have decided to choose myself.

I never aimed to impress people with a career or climb any ladder... but to hopefully inspire others to be who they are meant to be, fully and authentically.

My passion is to reconnect people with their gifts and soul and to believe in the magic of life again.

I now live in FNQ and offer private and public ceremonies, individual sessions of life coaching, spiritual and magical workshops as well as public speaking in Australia and in Europe.

MAGIC HAPPENS

RUDI LANDMANN

"Let me just get this," I said to the friend I was having lunch with. The number on my phone was unfamiliar, the kind that I would normally let go straight to voicemail, but something told me I should answer it.

"Hi, is that Rudi?" a woman asked. "Yes…"

"Hi. I'm from Camilla's team. We've got a show tomorrow and I was wondering whether you'd be willing to model for us?"

Someone from one of Australia's most prestigious fashion houses was asking me to walk for them? Well, excuse me while I check my diary…!

With my stomach all fluttery, I managed to compose myself to answer, "Of course! I'd be honoured. When do you need me to come in?"

And so began one of the most incredible experiences of my life.

A few months earlier, I had signed up to a runway modelling course as a way to build my self-confidence. It was a lot of fun and definitely gave me what I had wanted from it. I hadn't been sure of how or when I would ever use my new skills on an actual runway, but that hadn't been the point. Now, however, I was being cast in an actual show, and with a label I absolutely adored.

But why did they come looking for *me*, an absolute novice and nobody? Well, as I later learned, I had attracted some attention as someone who had loved the brand for years and was known around town for constantly wearing the label and tagging it on social media. So, when the show organisers realised they needed more diversity on the runway, I was already top of mind.

To explain why "diversity" is a factor here, I need to backtrack a little. I am not a typical *Camilla* customer. The extraverted Sydney label with its diaphanous, colourful kaftans and floaty, crystal-encrusted silk dresses is definitely not to everyone's taste. For addicts like me, however, nothing makes us feel more pretty, more feminine or more like an absolute goddess.

The main thing that sets me apart from most other aficionados is that I was born with a typically male body.

Our society makes a lot of assumptions about a person based on which "bits" they were born with. We presume to know a lot about someone's personality, likes and dislikes, hobbies, interests, what they might want to do with their life, what clothes they would like to wear what they're like to talk to, and a million other things large and small. Very little, if any, of this is determined by biological sex. "There is no gene for dress-wearing," I like to say. Instead, these assumptions form part of a set of rules we call *gender*, and we expect people with girl bits to behave according to the girl rules and people with boy bits to behave according to the boy rules.

But I was actually never very good at the role handed to me!

As a boy, I was *supposed* to love sport. But I was absolutely terrible at (and hated!) every single one to which Physical Education classes at school exposed me. And I could never quite figure out why I should care about which team on the TV was winning or why classmates would refer to their preferred team as "we", as if they themselves were playing. I'm probably among the least competitive people you could ever meet. But

AUTHENTICITY & ACTION

watching ballet? That's something I fell in love with before I was ten years old.

I was *supposed* to like noisy, violent, fast-paced movies, but these mostly seemed pointless and shallow to me at best, and actually distressing to watch, at worst. I much preferred to watch something sweet and romantic; something that made my heart melt.

I was *supposed* to be bold and assertive -- to take up space. But I'm softly spoken, well spoken, and the person always being talked over in conversations or meetings, often unable to get a word in. And eventually, as an adult living in a large male body, I was always somehow invisible while waiting to be served at the bar.

On the other hand, I was *not supposed* to express deep feelings, or to love bright colours and pretty things, or want to co-ordinate fun outfits and help style my friends. Nor to read what women wrote about and listen to what they sang about. And I certainly wasn't *supposed* to feel so strongly connected to my mother and grandmother or have female heroes and role-models. In my twenties, when I made a mix-tape (remember those?) for a woman I was getting to know, her first reaction the next time we met was, "They're all women!" I hadn't even noticed; these were just my favourite singers, the ones who spoke to me.

In most ways, I was very bad at being a boy!

The problem is, gender not only describes how we are all expected to live, but the way many people will try to *compel* us to live. For a vast number of transgender people around the world, this compulsion has extended to some people not letting us live at all.

Whether we agree with our society's gender rules or not, we all know what they are and know the potential consequences of breaking them. In my early forties, I reached a turning point, and it was a piece of fashion that broke the camel's back: a pair of tights by Lorna Jane, the iconic Australian women's activewear label.

I had recently embarked on a project to get fit and healthy. I discovered that, despite what school had taught me, I *didn't* hate exercise and physical activity, only what had been on offer at the time. I discovered I loved social running (thanks parkrun!), I had learned to ride a bike, and most of all, I discovered I absolutely loved group fitness classes at my local gym; the dance-ier the better!

One night, as I walked past a Lorna Jane, I noticed a pair of beautiful tights in the window, adorned with stars and constellations. It was love at first sight! But…these were women's tights, right? And I remember feeling sad that they were not for me.

I couldn't put them out of my head, and a few days later, I just had to buy them. I found the name of the print online, figured out my size, and then stammered my way through buying them "for my wife", as I explained to the shop assistant. I'm sure I blushed as I declined the upsell of the matching bra.

The next Saturday, I wanted to wear them on a social run. I literally put them on and changed out of them three times before I worked up the nerve to venture out of my house in them. I loved how they looked and felt on me, yet I felt very anxious and afraid.

To my great relief, it turned out to be a massive anticlimax. Nobody looked at me askance, nobody said anything mean or rude, and the only comments at all were positive ones from my female friends about how much they loved them or how well I wore them. This experience has stuck with me as a powerful reminder that our fears about what *might* happen can severely limit our ability to live authentically. Reality rarely aligns with our worst-case scenarios.

Now that the floodgates were open, I quickly found other Lorna Jane prints to love, and soon, wearing these pretty tights became my everyday running and exercise style. I started to wonder what this might mean.

Humans develop language and vocabulary to talk about our world, and every group or community inevitably develops its own way to talk about shared experiences. Trans and gender-diverse people sometimes use the metaphor of an egg cracking to describe our journey of self-discovery. Noting the joy I experienced from expressing femininity through clothing, put a big crack in my egg. Suddenly, I started to look at my life and question myself.

Many people seem to imagine that someone decides "I identify as trans" and then sets out to change their life to fit that choice. In fact, the process is almost always the opposite; eventually the sum total of our lived experiences bring us to a place where we consider all the cracks in our egg, look at a label like "trans" or "non-binary" and ask ourselves "is this who I am?"

The question then becomes whether we are brave enough to explore those feelings further, regardless of where that might take us. For me, it became a question of trying out other little pieces of traditionally feminine presentation to see what it felt like to present to the world that way. Would the outward expression be a more authentic representation of how I felt inside?

And every little change I made in my presentation felt good, and right, and brought me joy. The conclusion was inescapable; the further I let go of the need to conform to masculinity and embraced femininity instead, the happier I was.

There's a quote I love by Elizabeth Appell (often misattributed to Anaïs Nin): "And the day came when the risk to remain tight in a bud was more painful than the risk it took to blossom."

It should not be risky for anyone to fit into society however they want, without hurting others. If I feel pretty with painted nails, that should be nobody's concern but my own. In general, I think that the world would be a far better place if fewer people were ready to yell at others "Hey! Stop living your life differently from how I like to live mine!" But this unsolicited and unwelcome advice is everywhere.

Sometimes, people's disapproval of others' lives takes the form of *literal* yelling or physical intimidation, and there's the risk.

"Ooooh, nice tights, mate!" one of the men squealed in a mocking falsetto. "Is that a DUDE????" another chimed in.

"Leth go, girlth!" lisped a third, reading the words on my T-shirt as he lunged into my path, causing me to quickly sidestep to avoid a collision. Keeping my eyes downcast, I quickened my pace to hurry past them, laughter and catcalls ringing in my ears. Any moment, I expected to feel hands grab at me, but thankfully, that moment didn't come.

My world has changed in many ways since I first started venturing out of the house in clothes, shoes and accessories that our society's gender rules say only people with female bodies are permitted to wear. Out of all of these changes, the loss of a sense of personal safety has been the most profound. For most of my life, most of my closest friends have been women. And so, of course, I have always known about and believed women's concerns about the need to stay alert to their physical surroundings. Being six feet tall and weighing over 100 kg for most of my adult life, that's something I literally never had to worry about! It seems incredible to me now, but I spent decades obliviously wandering through the world with literally not a single thought for my surroundings. Now, I am at least as vigilant as any woman, and often afraid. I too worry if I'm alone at night and see a group of men walking in my direction. I too now cross the street, or at least avoid eye contact, as I hurry past. I too sometimes hear them laugh at and rejoice in the discomfort and fear they have caused.

And that's not to mention the online hate that's regularly directed my way. When I posted on social media to say how much I missed my mother on Mother's Day, someone took time out of their day to tell me:

"That's not a reason to go around claiming you are a woman. Get

AUTHENTICITY & ACTION

therapy and stop throwing women under a bus because your mom died."

Just this week, two people have used social media to tell me that people *like me* should not be allowed to live, with one offering to end my life himself.

It greatly puzzles me when some people claim that others' gender or sexuality is only ever a choice or fad or trend. Why would anyone choose to expose themselves to the cruelty of strangers this way?

I think this is the pivotal question for anyone seeking to live an authentic life. Because it doesn't matter whether we defy others' expectations and opinions in a big, whole-of-life way, or in something as relatively minor as a hairstyle that happens to make us happy. There's always a solid chance that somebody, somewhere is going to tell us that *we're doing life wrong.*

Be very selective who you listen to, because none of us really have time to waste.

By the time I was in my mid-30s, most of the people I had loved most of all in the world were dead. The life cut most short was my youngest brother. He died a few weeks short of his 32nd birthday when his heart suddenly stopped; a known but extremely rare side-effect of a prescription medication he was on.

And the blessing from all the pain and loss I've known has been a very real and ever-present sense that life is short and fragile; that none of us is guaranteed a tomorrow. Knowing that, why would we not want to live as authentically as we can, as joyfully as we can.

In one of her works, the poet Mary Oliver asks us, "Tell me, what is it you plan to do with your one wild and precious life?"

Given the limited time available, we must choose wisely.

The day I strutted out onto a Camilla runway was one of the happiest of my life; a real peak experience. I could hear the cheers of friends and supporters, and I was so happy and so proud to be representing a label I loved, but which also loved and supported me that day.

And right there in the audience watching and cheering me on? Lorna Jane Clarkson and her team. When I received a text from them a few weeks later asking if I'd like to appear in two upcoming promotions for her label, I felt that I'd come full circle in a way, and that by having the courage to express my authentic self, magic had truly happened.

RUDI LANDMANN

Rudi is many things: a pilates, breathwork, and meditation teacher, life coach, cuddle therapist, consent educator, diversity educator, and runway model!

As a non-binary person, Rudi moves through the world as feminine and uses the pronouns they/them. They have had the privilege of working with major brands including Camilla, Lorna Jane, Dissh, and Proud Poppy, and with many emerging Australian designers.

They have walked on multiple runways in Brisbane and Sydney, including the Camilla Spring/Summer 2022 launch, Ravishing Fashionistas, Rise to the Runway, Queensland Arts and Fashion Festival, and the Australia-Brazil Chamber of Commerce fashion days.

In their professional practice, Rudi coaches women on getting their sparkle back when it feels like life has dulled it down.

They also work with large and small organisations on how to be more welcoming to their LGBTQIA+ clients,

They were the proud recipient of the 2023 Special Recognition award by Women's Network Australia, and the 2024 Courageous Leadership award from Boss Ladies.

Rudi's dream is to help make the world a better and kinder place by

RUDI LANDMANN

building understanding and connection, and to see every woman flourishing and radiant in her power.

UNMASKING THE TRUTH

REDISCOVERING MY IDENTITY

SARA KNIGHT

This piece is a deeply personal reflection on my journey of unmasking as an autistic individual. It is my perspective, shaped by my unique experiences and challenges, and it may not reflect the journey of others on the spectrum. Autism is a vast and varied spectrum and no two experiences are exactly alike. My story is just one among many and I share it, not as a universal truth, but as an honest account of how I've navigated the complexities of my neurodivergence, motherhood and mental health. My hope is that this will resonate with those who have walked a similar path and foster understanding among those who seek to learn.

For years, I lived in a world where I felt out of sync, as though I were a visitor navigating an alien planet, desperately trying to blend in. The energy it took to 'mask' my authentic self was monumental, yet I didn't even know it had a name. It wasn't until I was diagnosed with autism that I began to understand my journey and how profoundly *masking* had shaped my life.

My earliest memories of masking trace back to my childhood. My mother would often insist I look her in the eyes when speaking to her. She equated eye contact with honesty, and if I struggled to maintain it, she would accuse me of lying. (The consequences you don't wish to imagine.) The act felt unnatural, even painful, as though I was being forced to hold a burning stare. Yet, to avoid conflict and the sting of being labelled *untruthful*, I complied, practicing a skill that would become a cornerstone of my masking behaviour. Over time, I learned to mimic this and other social norms, but the underlying discomfort never went away. You see, girls in my generation didn't have autism - it was barely a possible thought. I learned *to do* eye contact, or at least what people thought was eye contact, as a need to survive. Even today, people expect it. *Sigh*.

I sensed I was different but didn't have the language to articulate it. I found solace in the quiet corners of the library or spent hours immersed in creative pursuits, losing myself in art, school, books and storytelling. These were my refuges, the places where my vibrant inner world could thrive. Yet, in social settings, I felt the need to suppress my natural inclinations. I studied people's behaviours, mimicked their expressions and rehearsed social scripts to fit in. Every interaction became a performance, carefully curated to avoid standing out.

My journey has also been deeply intertwined with my experience as a survivor of domestic and family violence. That chapter of my life was marked by a different kind of masking - one born of survival rather than social expectation. In those years, masking became a shield; a way to protect myself and my child from further harm. I became adept at hiding my pain, projecting an image of strength and normalcy even as I endured unspeakable hardships. It was a role I played out of necessity, but it left deep scars.

This masking - a term I later learned to describe the act of concealing one's autistic traits to conform to societal expectations - felt like wearing an ill-fitting costume. It was heavy and suffocating, but I thought it was necessary. I didn't yet realise the toll it was taking on my mental health and self-esteem.

AUTHENTICITY & ACTION

My journey began in earnest when I became a mother. Motherhood is transformative for anyone, but for me, it was also a mirror - one that revealed the parts of myself I had long hidden. As my children grew, I noticed behaviours in them that felt deeply familiar. Their sensitivity to sound, their unique ways of expressing joy, their struggles with certain social expectations. It was as if I were looking at a reflection of my younger self. When they were diagnosed with autism, it became impossible to ignore the parallels. Their diagnoses were a revelation that ultimately led me to seek my own.

When I received my autism diagnosis at age twenty-eight, it was like finding the missing piece of a puzzle I had been trying to solve my entire life. Suddenly, everything made sense; my sensitivity to sensory input, my intense focus on interests, my need for structure and predictability. But alongside the relief came grief, for the years I had spent suppressing these traits, believing they were flaws.

As I processed my diagnosis, I began to see the ways in which masking had affected my life. It wasn't just the exhaustion from constantly pretending to be someone I wasn't. It was also the relationships I had lost because I couldn't sustain the façade, the opportunities I had missed because I feared being 'found out' and the deep sense of disconnection from myself.

Unmasking has been both liberating and terrifying. It's a process of peeling away layers of self-protection and facing the vulnerability underneath. I've had to confront the internalised ableism that told me I needed to be normal to be worthy of love and respect. I've had to reframe my understanding of success, shifting from external validation to internal fulfillment.

It has not been without its challenges. Society often rewards conformity and punishes difference, and the fear of judgment can be paralysing. The pressure to adhere to societal norms creates an invisible weight, like you're in a machine that's compressing your nervous system; one that feels even heavier when compounded by the lack of understanding about autism. There have been moments when I've hesitated to share my story, worried about how it might be received. Would people see me differently? Would they judge my abilities or dismiss my achievements? These questions lingered, feeding a cycle of self-doubt that was hard to break, allowing my own mental health to win for a little bit.

For me, it was not a singular event but a gradual process, like peeling back layers that had been built up over a lifetime. It started with small, deliberate acts of authenticity, allowing myself to stim freely, speaking up about sensory challenges and no longer forcing eye contact when it felt uncomfortable. I stopped apologising for needing downtime after social interactions and began openly sharing my experiences as an autistic individual. Each step felt both terrifying and liberating, as though I were stepping into the light after years in the shadows. What truly cemented my unmasking was embracing my creativity as a reflection of my neurodivergence, allowing my photography and storytelling to be unapologetically shaped by how I see the world. Through unmasking, I have reclaimed my identity, showing up as my true self in a world that once demanded I hide.

Over time, I've come to realise that vulnerability is a strength, not a weakness. By being open about my autism, I've found a sense of community and connection I never thought possible. Sharing my story has brought me closer to others who have had similar experiences, creating bonds that transcend the superficial and delve into the heart of human connection. The support I've received has been a powerful reminder that authenticity resonates far more deeply than perfection ever could.

Breaking free from that environment required immense courage and it taught me the value of self-advocacy and resilience. Escaping wasn't just a physical act, it was a reclamation of my identity and autonomy. It

AUTHENTICITY & ACTION

meant unlearning the lies I had been told about my worth and rebuilding a sense of self from the ground up. This process was both painful and empowering, forcing me to confront the parts of myself I had buried under layers of fear and shame.

In many ways, my experience as a survivor has informed my unmasking journey. It has given me a profound understanding of the importance of self-compassion and the strength it takes to live authentically. It has also fuelled my desire to create safe spaces for others, whether through my work, friendship or my storytelling. I know what it's like to feel invisible, to hide behind a mask because the world doesn't feel safe. And I know the transformative power of being seen and accepted for who you truly are.

Today, I channel these lessons into my work. As a photographer, I strive to create spaces where my clients feel seen and valued for who they truly are. My neurodivergent perspective allows me to capture moments of genuine connection and emotion and my lived experience helps me empathise with the challenges they may face. Through my children's books and co-authoring with others, I aim to inspire young and old readers to embrace their differences and celebrate their unique strengths.

Social media has been another powerful tool in my unmasking journey. Social media platforms have allowed me to share not only my professional work but also glimpses of my personal story. At first, I was hesitant to be so vulnerable online, but the response has been overwhelmingly positive. People resonate with authenticity and by sharing my struggles and triumphs, I've been able to foster a sense of community among my followers.

One of the most rewarding aspects of this journey has been the opportunity to advocate for greater understanding and acceptance of autism. Through my work, I hope to challenge stereotypes and misconceptions, showing that autism is not a limitation but a different way of experiencing the world. By sharing my perspective, I aim to create a ripple effect, encouraging others to embrace their true selves and support those around them in doing the same.

The act of unmasking has also redefined my relationships. By embracing my myself, I have attracted people into my life who value and accept me for who I truly am. This shift has been profound, moving from connections based on convenience or societal expectations to relationships rooted in mutual understanding and genuine care. These bonds have shown me the beauty of vulnerability; how it creates space for deeper connections and fosters an environment of trust and acceptance.

Unmasking remains an ongoing process. There are days when the old patterns resurface, when the temptation to conform feels overwhelming. It can be exhausting to constantly advocate for myself and my children, as well as educate others about autism, all while resisting the urge to slip back into the comfort of masking. But each time, I remind myself of the freedom that authenticity brings. I remind myself of the joy of being fully seen and fully accepted - not just by others, but by myself.

This journey has also inspired me to reflect on the societal structures that demand masking in the first place. Why is difference so often met with resistance rather than curiosity? Why are individuals pressured to conform to norms that stifle their unique perspectives? These questions fuel my advocacy work, pushing me to challenge these norms and create spaces where diversity is celebrated rather than merely tolerated.

In my work, I have witnessed the power of authenticity firsthand. When clients feel safe to let their guard down, to be themselves in front of the camera, the results are breathtaking. There's a raw beauty in capturing people as they truly are; in their joy, their vulnerability, their complexity. These moments remind me why unmasking matters, because our true selves are worth celebrating.

I hope to plant the seeds of acceptance and empathy in the next generation. By telling stories that celebrate difference and resilience, I

AUTHENTICITY & ACTION

aim to create a world where children feel empowered to be themselves. My children's books are more than just stories, they are messages of hope and encouragement for anyone who has ever felt out of place.

The path of unmasking is not linear. It is a journey filled with setbacks and triumphs, with moments of doubt and clarity. But it is a journey worth taking. Each step brings me closer to a life that feels truly mine - a life where I am not just surviving but thriving. It is a life where my differences are not just accepted but celebrated, where my story inspires others to embrace their own.

For those who are just beginning their unmasking journey, I offer this: be patient with yourself. Unmasking is not about rushing to reveal everything at once, it is about taking small, deliberate steps toward authenticity. Surround yourself with people who uplift you, who see your worth even when you struggle to see it yourself. And remember, your journey is uniquely yours. There is no right or wrong way to unmask - only the way that feels right for you.

As I continue to unmask, I carry with me the lessons of my past. I carry the resilience forged in the fires of adversity, the creativity that flows from my neurodivergent mind and the love that fuels everything I do. I carry the hopes and dreams of the little girl who once hid in her bedroom and within herself, dreaming of a world where she could be herself. And I carry the knowledge that authenticity is not just a gift to myself but to everyone I meet.

Unmasking is not just about revealing who I am, it's about reclaiming my power and creating a space where others can do the same. It's about finding beauty in the imperfections and strength in the struggle. And it's about living a life that is unapologetically, authentically mine - even in the face of adversity.

As I reflect on this journey, I am reminded of Brené Brown's words: *Authenticity is the daily practice of letting go of who we think we're supposed to be and embracing who we are.*

These words resonate deeply with me because unmasking is, at its core, a practice; a deliberate and courageous choice I make every day. It is a choice to honour my truth, to embrace my neurodivergence and to celebrate the resilience that has carried me through, not just for myself but for you and others like you.

My story is far from over and I know there will be challenges ahead. But I also know that the freedom to live as my true self is worth every step of the journey. And as we each unmask, we create a world that is richer, more compassionate and more accepting for all.

Unmasking is not just a personal journey, it's a collective call for change. When we, as individuals, embrace our true selves and share our stories, we create ripples of understanding and compassion. By joining together as a united front, we challenge outdated norms, shatter harmful stereotypes and pave the way for a world where authenticity is celebrated, not feared.

In unity, we find strength. Together, we can build a society that values diversity; one where differences are not just accepted but cherished. And in doing so, we create a brighter future - not just for ourselves, but for the generations to come. Let us stand together, hand in hand, as a testament to the power of vulnerability, resilience and unwavering hope.

There is strength in vulnerability, beauty in difference and power in authenticity.

SARA KNIGHT

Sara Louise is a 39-year-old, accomplished photographer and mum of six. She is the creative force behind Sara Louise Photography; a thriving business known for its captivating and evocative images. Based in Australia, Sara's journey in photography has been marked by both personal triumphs and professional accolades, reflecting her resilience, talent and unyielding passion for the art form.

As an individual with autism with CPTSD and a survivor of domestic and family violence, she found solace and expression through the lens of her camera. Photography became a powerful medium for her to communicate her unique perspective and experiences, allowing her to connect with others in profound ways. This personal connection to her work is evident in the emotive quality of her photographs, which resonate with viewers around the world.

Sara's artistry has earned global recognition, including the prestigious International Street Photographer of the Year 2023/2024 award. Her work has been showcased worldwide and she has been a finalist in several high-profile awards, including the BX Awards, the Mono Awards and the Australian Ladies in Business Initiative. She was also honoured with the 'Overcoming the Odds' category by the Australian Ladies in Business

SARA KNIGHT

Initiative, celebrating her extraordinary journey as an autistic survivor of domestic and family violence.

Sara's photography is characterised by a keen eye for detail, a deep understanding of light and shadow, and an innate ability to capture fleeting moments of emotion and connection. Her portfolio is diverse, ranging from striking street photography to intimate portraits and evocative landscapes. Each photograph is a testament to her dedication to the craft and her unwavering commitment to producing work of the highest quality.

Beyond her professional achievements, Sara is also a passionate advocate for mental health awareness and domestic violence survivors. She uses her platform to raise awareness and inspire others, sharing her story to empower those who may be facing similar challenges. Her advocacy work is an integral part of her mission, underscoring her belief in the transformative power of art and storytelling and another reason to share who she is by authoring or co-authoring in books.

Sara Louise Photography has not only become a recognised name in the industry but also a symbol of resilience and hope. With a growing clientele and a portfolio that continues to expand, Sara's future in photography looks incredibly bright. Her journey is a testament to the strength of the human spirit and the power of art to heal, inspire and connect us all.

AUTHENTICITY ARCHITECTURE

YOUR SPARKLY RESET

TANYA HICKS

Think about your life for a moment. Does it feel uniquely yours, or does it feel like you're living according to someone else's script?

From an early age, we are handed blueprints - plans filled with expectations, definitions of success and rigid paths to follow. Study hard. Get a "good" job. Build a family. Work tirelessly. Retire comfortably. On the surface, these steps seem like the foundation for a well-lived life.

But have you ever paused to ask yourself: *Whose blueprint is this?*

For years, I didn't question the plan. I followed it with unwavering dedication, constructing my metaphorical house with precision. I painted the walls with bright successes, filled the rooms with achievements and polished the surfaces to appear perfect. Yet something felt off. Inside, the rooms felt suffocating, the furnishings foreign. I had built a house, but it wasn't a home - it was a facade.

This realisation hit me like a tidal wave one quiet afternoon, as I watched my son play. He sat on the floor, arranging his dolls into meticulous rows. His humming radiated a joy so pure it was almost otherworldly. Watching him, I saw something undeniable - a reflection of myself. His authenticity forced me to confront my own lack of it.

At that moment, I realised I wasn't just following someone else's blueprint; I had built my life on their terms. The bright paint, the sturdy walls, the carefully curated details - it all reflected what I thought I *should* do, not who I really was. And for the first time, I asked myself: *What would it feel like to live authentically?*

This isn't just a philosophical question. Living authentically isn't a luxury or a distant dream, it's a necessity. When we live out of alignment with ourselves, we feel it everywhere; in our work, our relationships, and even our well-being. It dulls our joy and dims our spark. But authenticity creates flow. It allows us to move through life with greater ease, to experience a deeper sense of purpose, and to truly connect, with ourselves and with others.

This chapter is your invitation to create what I call your *Sparkly Reset*. It's a chance to break free from a life designed by external expectations and start building a life that feels like home.

IDENTIFYING THE CRACKS IN YOUR BLUEPRINT

We often don't notice the cracks in our blueprints until life forces us to. For me, it was a moment of seeing someone I love live in complete, unapologetic authenticity. Watching them embrace who they were - without hesitation or fear - made me realise how much of myself I had been suppressing.

The cracks in your blueprint might look different. Maybe it's the job that pays the bills but drains your soul. Perhaps it's relationships where you constantly compromise your needs. Or it could be the relentless pursuit of perfection that leaves you feeling hollow.

These cracks aren't failures; they're invitations. They whisper: *Something isn't right. Let's reconnect and rebuild.*

Take a moment to reflect:

What areas of your life feel misaligned?

Where do you feel stuck, drained or out of place?

What parts of yourself have you been hiding to fit in?

AUTHENTICITY & ACTION

Recognising the cracks is the first step toward your *Sparkly Reset*. It's not about tearing everything down - it's about carefully examining what feels off and deciding what's worth keeping.

For example, you might realise you've been staying in a career that looks great on paper but leaves you feeling unfulfilled. Perhaps you've been holding onto friendships that drain your energy instead of nurturing your soul. These realisations can be uncomfortable, even painful, but they're also empowering. They're the foundation of change.

When I started this process, I realised that much of what I had built wasn't even mine. The expectations I lived by belonged to others - family, society, culture. It wasn't easy to confront, but it was liberating.

This process isn't about self-criticism. It's about self-awareness. Each crack you uncover is an opportunity to bring your life closer to what truly matters to *you*.

Now, I invite you to take out a piece of paper or open a blank document. Write down the areas of your life where you feel those cracks. Be honest and specific. This exercise isn't about fixing everything immediately, it's about creating clarity.

Your *Sparkly Reset* begins with this step: acknowledging the cracks and choosing to see them as invitations for growth, freedom and alignment.

YOUR SPARKLY RESET PHILOSOPHY

Your *Sparkly Reset* is more than just a concept. It's a philosophy - a way of living that prioritises authenticity, personal truth and joy. It's about honouring who you are, your quirks, your values and your individuality - without apology.

A. Reclaim Your Joy

Joy isn't frivolous; it's foundational.

Think back to the last time you felt truly alive. Was it during a creative project? A moment of stillness in nature? A time when you fully expressed yourself without fear of judgment? Joy isn't something to chase - it's something to follow. It's your internal compass, guiding you toward the life that feels most like *home*.

Reclaiming joy often requires unlearning. Many of us were taught that joy must be *earned*, that it's a reward for hard work, productivity or success. But joy isn't a transaction; it's a right.

For me, reclaiming joy meant moving in ways that connected me back to myself. Yoga became my grounding force, while surfing pushed me out of my comfort zone, reminding me of the exhilaration of rising after every fall. And there were *many* falls!

What brings you joy? What lights you up? Give yourself permission to follow it.

B. Redefine Success

Society often defines success through titles, wealth, and accolades - and to be honest, I've had my fair share of those. But at some point, I had to ask myself: *Do these things actually fulfill me?*

True success isn't about ticking off external milestones, it's about living in a way that reflects your values.

Ask yourself:

What does success mean to *you*?

Is it about financial security, creative freedom, meaningful relationships or something else entirely?

How do you want to feel at the end of each day?

There's no universal definition of success. The only measure that matters is the one *you* choose.

C. Cultivate Authentic Connections

Authenticity invites deeper, more fulfilling relationships. When you stop

AUTHENTICITY & ACTION

pretending, when you show up as you truly are, you create space for the kind of connections that nourish your soul.

Not every relationship will survive this process. And that's okay. Authenticity is a filter. Some relationships will grow stronger, while others may fall away. This can feel painful, but it's also *liberating*. The relationships that remain will be built on genuine connection, mutual respect and shared values.

Your *Sparkly Reset* isn't about drastic overhauls or tearing down everything you've built. It's about small, intentional shifts that move you closer to a life that feels fully *yours*.

BUILDING YOUR AUTHENTICITY ARCHITECTURE

Your *Sparkly Reset* begins with recognising the cracks, but the real magic happens when you start rebuilding. This is your Authenticity Architecture - the framework for a life designed by *you*.

Building this framework doesn't happen overnight, but it doesn't have to be overwhelming either. Think of it as laying one brick at a time, each intentional choice forming the foundation of a life that feels like home.

A. Know Your Core Values

Your values are the cornerstone of your *Authenticity Architecture*. They are your internal compass, guiding your decisions and shaping a life that truly reflects what matters most to you.

Often, we inherit values from our upbringing, society or culture, without questioning whether they align with who we really are. But living authentically requires defining your own.

Take a moment to reflect:

What truly lights you up?

What qualities do you admire in others?

What are you unwilling to compromise on?

What brings you joy?

What do you stand for?

What do you want *more* of in your life?

Write down your top five values. Keep them somewhere visible, on your phone, your mirror or in a journal. Use them as a filter for your decisions, both big and small. When your actions align with your values, you create a life that feels authentic, fulfilling and deeply yours.

B. Designing a Life That Reflects Your Blueprint

Getting clear about your values is like finding your internal compass. It brings clarity in a world full of distractions.

Once you've identified your core values, take an honest look at how you spend your time.

Does your daily life reflect what you truly value?

Are your priorities in alignment with the things that bring you joy, peace, and meaning?

If family is important to you but your schedule is dominated by work, it may be time to recalibrate. If creativity fuels your soul but your days are filled with tasks that drain you, carve out space for expression.

Aligning your life with your values doesn't mean perfection, it means intentionality. Even small shifts can create profound changes, helping you live a life that feels authentic, sustainable, and fulfilling.

C. Create Rituals That Support You

Rituals anchor you to your authenticity. They're not just habits, they're intentional practices that nurture your body, mind and soul.

For me, movement rituals like yoga and surfing became my sanctuary. They reminded me to connect with my body, embrace life's natural flow and return to myself - over and over again.

AUTHENTICITY & ACTION

The Power of Rituals:

- *Rituals Create Stability & Safety*

Life is unpredictable, but rituals create a sense of structure and stability in the chaos.

When practiced consistently, they provide a safe container for growth and reflection.

- *Rituals Enhance Mindfulness & Presence*

Intentional practices like meditation, breathwork or mindful walks help reduce mental clutter and foster clarity.

These practices engage the parasympathetic nervous system (the "rest and digest" state), lowering stress and promoting well-being.

- *Rituals Strengthen Positive Neural Pathways*

The brain adapts based on repetition—the more we engage in supportive rituals, the more automatic they become.

Over time, rituals rewire the brain for resilience, clarity and emotional well-being.

- *Rituals Align Your Body & Mind*

Movement-based rituals (yoga, dance, running, swimming) release endorphins and regulate mood.

These activities also stimulate brain-derived neurotrophic factor (BDNF), which supports learning and cognitive function.

- *Rituals Reinforce Identity & Authenticity*

    When you choose rituals that reflect your values, you affirm who you are. This alignment strengthens self-trust and fosters a deep sense of purpose.

How to Create & Maintain Effective Rituals:

- *Start Small & Specific*

    Choose *one* ritual to begin with and set a simple, specific practice.
    Example: A 10-minute journaling session each morning if writing helps you process emotions.

- *Connect to Your Why*

    Understand *why* this ritual is important to you.
    Example: Yoga might ground you, while painting might bring you joy and creativity.

- *Stack It with an Existing Habit*

    Link a new ritual to something you already do.
    Example: Meditate for five minutes right after brushing your teeth.

- *Embrace Flexibility*

    Rituals should serve you - not become another source of stress. Allow room for adjustments based on your energy and needs.

- *Reflect on the Impact*

AUTHENTICITY & ACTION

Regularly check in: *Does this ritual still support you?*

Adjust as needed to ensure it continues to nourish and uplift you.

By incorporating intentional rituals into your life, you create a framework for self-nurturance, clarity and deep connection with yourself.

These practices are not just routines, they are tools for transformation, helping you design a life that feels fully, unapologetically yours.

D. Declutter Your Emotional Space

Just as we declutter our homes, we must also declutter our emotional spaces.

This doesn't mean removing everything or everyone from your life, it means getting intentional about what supports your well-being and what drains it.

Ask yourself:

What lifts my energy?

What drains my energy?

Where do I feel peace, ease and alignment?

Where do I feel tension, resistance or depletion?

You don't have to have all the answers right away. Noticing is the first step.

Here's your reminder: We can do hard things. If something no longer supports the life you're building, it's okay to release it with love.

TAKING ACTION WITH YOUR SPARKLY RESET

Your *Sparkly Reset* isn't just about reflection, it's about action.

Small, consistent steps hold the power to create profound transformation.

1. Start Small

Your *Sparkly Reset* doesn't require grand gestures or overnight changes. Begin with one area of your life.

Maybe it's:

Setting boundaries in a relationship.

Incorporating a daily mindfulness practice.
Dedicating 10 minutes a day to something that brings you joy.
Each small step matters. Progress is always more powerful than perfection.
Celebrate every win, no matter how small.

2. Embrace the Power of Learning & Adapting
Authenticity isn't a destination, it's a process. Along the way, you'll try things that work and things that don't - and that's okay.

Each step, even the uncertain ones, is an opportunity to recalibrate.

When I first started living more authentically, I worried about how others would perceive me. Some people didn't understand, and that was hard.

But I reminded myself: *This isn't about meeting expectations, it's about living truthfully.*

You don't need to have everything figured out. You just need to keep moving forward in ways that feel true to you.

3. Build Your Support Network
Authenticity thrives in community.

Surround yourself with people who:

- Celebrate your uniqueness.
- Encourage your growth.
- Support you without expectation.

This might mean:

- Leaning on friends who uplift you.
- Joining a group of like-minded individuals.
- Seeking out mentors or role models who inspire you.
- If you're anything like me, you might need all three!

AUTHENTICITY & ACTION

- Your support network is the scaffolding that holds up your *Authenticity Architecture*. You don't have to do this alone.

Designing a Life That Feels Like Home (and is Super Sparkly!)
The journey to authenticity isn't linear or easy but it's worth every step.

When you create your *Sparkly Reset*, you reclaim your joy, redefine success and build a life that truly feels like home.

For me? That home became lit up with fairy lights 365 days per year - but hey, *you do you!*

Now, imagine waking up each day feeling:

- Aligned with your values.
- Connected to your passions.
- Surrounded by relationships that nurture your soul.

That's the promise of Your *Sparkly Reset* - a life that isn't just built for you but by you.

As you embark on this journey, remember:

- You don't have to have it all figured out.
- Start with one small step.
- One intentional choice.
- One brave moment of stepping into yourself.
- Over time, these small actions will transform your life in ways you can't yet imagine.

Your Authenticity Architecture is waiting to be built.
Your Sparkly Reset is the blueprint.
Time to begin.

TANYA HICKS

T anya Hicks is an award-winning leader, advocate and author of *The Sparkly Alien Empowerment Series*, a transformative collection of books designed to help individuals and communities thrive through authenticity, connection and self-discovery. As *The Sparkly Alien*, Tanya inspires others to break free from external expectations, embrace their unique brilliance, and design lives that feel truly their own.

A proud late-identified neurodivergent woman, Tanya is passionate about creating a world where authenticity is celebrated and where those who have felt like they don't belong can step into their fullest expression with joy and confidence.

A Defining "Not on My Watch" Moment

Tanya's journey into advocacy took a pivotal turn when her son was diagnosed as autistic at the age of two. During assessments, a psychologist revealed a sobering truth; his exceptional intelligence placed him at a high risk of becoming suicidal as a teenager due to the disconnect between himself and his peers.

This became Tanya's defining *"Not on my watch"* moment.

Determined to create a life where her son could thrive, she restructured their world, transitioning from mainstream schooling to an unschooling approach that prioritised joy, individuality and a way of learning that truly fit his needs.

As she embraced her own neurodivergence, she discovered the power of unmasking, reclaiming joy and living authentically, not just for her son, but for herself. This journey led her to become *The Sparkly Alien*, a leader in radical self-acceptance, empowerment and the freedom to exist outside the world's rigid blueprints.

Championing Inclusion, Joy and Self-Acceptance

Tanya is dedicated to helping people shed expectations and reconnect with their own spark. She blends lived experience, professional expertise and an unshakable belief in human potential to create spaces where people are seen, valued and celebrated.

A former Australian Country hockey representative until the age of 31, she developed discipline, adaptability and resilience - qualities she now applies to her work as a clinical hypnotherapist and mindfulness yoga teacher. Her neurodivergent-affirming mindfulness practices combine science, compassion and innovation, offering individuals the tools to rediscover themselves, move with intention and build a life that aligns with who they truly are.

Founder of Neurodivergent Empowered

As the founder of Neurodivergent Empowered, Tanya has created a movement dedicated to empowerment, connection and building spaces where authenticity thrives.

Her organisation's initiatives include sensory-friendly programs, interest-based friendship groups and nervous system nourishment sessions, with over $190,000 in pro bono services for individuals without funding. Her work reflects her deep commitment to equity, accessibility and transformative impact.

Awards and Recognition

Tanya's impact has been recognised through numerous accolades,

AUTHENTICITY & ACTION

including:

2024 Stevie® Awards for Women in Business

Gold Global Winner – Children's Education – 2025 Women Changing The World Awards

Bronze Global Winner – Advocacy and Impact – 2025 Women Changing The World Awards

Gold Stevie Winner – Female Executive of the Year (Government or Non-Profit)

Silver Stevie Winner – Woman of the Year

Beam Awards 2024

Winner – Community Leader of the Year

AusMumpreneur Awards 2024

Winner – Overcoming the Odds Award

Global Recognition Award 2024

Winner – Significant Contributions to Supporting Neurodivergent Individuals and Their Families

Living a Sparkly, Authentic Life

Beyond her professional work, Tanya is a passionate advocate for nervous system nourishment, movement and holistic well-being. A perpetual "beginner" surfer, she finds joy in movement practices that connect the mind, body and soul. She lives her life lit with fairy lights 365 days a year … because why not?

Her story is a testament to the beauty of embracing imperfection, honouring individuality and living unapologetically.

Access Your Own Sparkly Reset

Visit www.thesparklyalien.com/books, search for *Authenticity and Action*, and use the password Authenticity&Action to unlock free resources designed to empower your journey toward your *Authenticity Architecture Sparkly Reset*.

FROM TRAGEDY TO PURPOSE IN MAKING AN IMPACT IN THE WORLD

WENDY SHEW

I believe that our purpose on this planet is to leave the world a better place than we found it – Robert Baden-Powell

I remember the morning I woke up in my cousin's room after all the aunts and uncles had spent the night at the hospital. I sat up in my sleeping bag on the floor from another sleepover at my cousin Alice's to find that my aunt was sitting there in front of us with tears in her eyes.

'Your mother passed last night.' I sat quietly - not surprised yet trying to comprehend what felt like the impossible. How does an eight-year-old comprehend death? And not just any death … but the most important relationship of her entire life.

At the time, I had no idea what it meant, but looking back, I can see how critical it was to shaping my life. The loss of my mother took away my meaning and feeling of safety. It took away the unconditional love of a mother that no one else could ever provide me.

The silver lining was that there were also three very great lessons my mother's passing taught me;

- that we must live out every dream
- the power of compassion; and lastly,
- the only legacy we leave behind is the positive impact we make on someone's life.

During the journey of my mother being sick, I remember her starting out at Chinese Hospital. As my father was pulling into the hospital, one of my mother's five sisters turned to me and told me that there were four stages of Cancer and my mother was currently in 'stage 4'. As an eight-year-old at the time, I really had no idea how to understand the depth of what she was trying to tell me.

A few weeks later, I remember leaving the hospital thinking it was such a depressing place to be. I watched as my mother got weaker and weaker, lost all her hair, had challenges breathing and, then, was barely able to speak. My father then took us to the fish store at the corner of Stockton in Chinatown … and he chose three turtles. This was the type of fish store where you could select your fish to cook and eat. We took those three live turtles and drove them down to Golden Gate Park, where there was a small pond. We released them into the park; three lives saved. That was the moment my father taught me the power of compassion, that no matter what is going on in life, if we have the capacity to help or save someone, we should do it.

I remember the days of watching my mother sitting on the sofa during her sickness, silent and unable to move, probably lost in her own thoughts of mortality. There was a spiritual therapist who came to visit and I remember how she would tell my mother to keep believing and fighting, that hope was a great power, and how if we stayed positive things could change.

The day she died, I realised that no one in the world was coming to take her place and be the source of love I needed.

AUTHENTICITY & ACTION

While my sister and cousin spent days putting puzzles together, I insisted on watching *Wonder Woman*. She was my role model growing up. I adored the way that she was strong and capable, and could protect herself, but saw how she was a source of good to protect others against all the wrong in the world. She made me realise that no one was coming to save me and it was my job to put on my own invisible cape to save myself.

And that is what I did. I devoted myself to academics and became a straight-A student. During my lunch breaks, instead of hanging out with friends, I would go to the gym and practice tumbling after laying mats on the ground. Somehow, practicing gymnastics made me feel invincible; capable of protecting myself. I was able to do things with my body that weren't possible before. This became my source of inspiration and power.

After high school, I lacked direction from a mentor to make the right decisions on how to move forward in life. I came to a life-changing realisation that I needed purpose and meaning. The saviour that came to my rescue was, again, the fundamentals of education. I wondered how I could change my beliefs and feel empowered. Over the next few weeks, I decided I wanted to learn how to fly a plane, so I set out to study aviation. I enrolled into a University, moved to Southern California with all my belongings in my car. I would complete my education and learn to fly.

I believed education was the discipline and structure I needed to become a contributing member of society. Studying aviation and learning to fly taught me that I was capable and could accomplish anything I set my mind to. Soaring through the skies, my problems and the self-defeating thoughts in my mind seemed so far away. I felt like I could leave those limiting beliefs behind on the ground as soon as I took off into the wind. It was then that I realised that not even the skies were the limit, but beyond. Those were the years that taught me hustle, hard work, grit and a commitment to my dreams, as I balanced going to school full-time, working two jobs and flight school. It was the training I needed to become the person I am today, in pursuit of making a difference and an impact in the world. After completing a dual associates in aviation science and commercial flight, with a bachelors in aviation management, I was recruited into my first aviation job before graduating. I worked for an aviation company, managing consignments of jet engines, overseeing teardowns and supporting jet engine part sales. This utilised my natural talent in business while also fulfilling my interest in the science of jet engines and learning about complex systems. Within the second year, I supported the company to drive a significant revenue goal that marked a milestone in my career. It was a goal that I was pushing for months, yet I felt something lacking when I finally hit it. I didn't feel the overwhelm of achievement, as I had hoped I would. In the next few days, my CEO had lunch with me and asked me two simple questions; *What position did I want in the company?* And, *How much money did I want to make?* I didn't realise it then, but those were the wrong questions to ask because titles and money have never been my core values.

At the same time, on my personal development journey, I was taking a leadership course that challenged me to seek beyond my normal everyday life. The program asked me what my passions were and what I wanted to do that I didn't believe would be possible for me. It was during a weekend workshop when they asked us to say the first goal that came to mind, *without judging it.* What popped out of my mouth was, 'I'm going to quit my job by March 2015 and travel the world.' I was shocked by my own words. It was then, September 2014.

So, with that desire in mind, I began searching for something that I felt would make a difference in the world. The very first thing that popped into my mind was to travel to India and work in female empowerment. As a little girl, I had always been fascinated with India; the colours, the spices, the aromas that derived from such a culturally rich country. Upon

AUTHENTICITY & ACTION

doing my research, there was another country that came up for me, one that I had never heard of; Nepal.

As I researched further, I learned about sherpas, beautiful, terraced mountains and the Himalayas. I saw that there were opportunities to teach young, orphaned Tibetan monks. The idea of traveling to India to work at a girl's orphanage or teach English to young Tibetan monks fascinated me; it was a world beyond what I knew. Life really was beyond the sky's limits. Although I could not decide which opportunity I wanted, I decided to go with my initial passion; to volunteer at a girl's orphanage in India. I decided I would also fly to Nepal on my birthday just to visit the country … and that was what I did.

Arriving in India at the airport was invigorating. There was so much happening in one place. Everything was unfamiliar but I found it exotic. It was noisy with people chattering and cars honking non-stop. I waited for my assigned driver to collect me. I hopped into the car and we drove out of the city, into a more rural area towards Faridabad, where the orphanage was located.

Upon arriving at the girl's orphanage, I had no idea what to expect. There were a total of twelve girls there and I arrived as they were cleaning the house. They were excited to see me; someone who was a foreigner and someone to talk to. I was assigned a bed to sleep in at the top of the house, along with another volunteer who was there. It was late at night already and I sat on the bed with Anjali, the oldest girl in the house. I was feeling jet-lagged and dizzy, unfamiliar with this feeling at first, and Anjali was going on and on excitedly, asking me questions about living in California … if I was married and what I did for work. Her curiosity was insatiable. An hour went by and I went to bed thinking how I loved the energy of India. There was something in the air. Whether it was excitement or busyness, I couldn't quite identify it, but it was definitely something I was grateful to experience.

At 4am, I woke from jet lag and could not go back to sleep, but India was already awake. At dawn, there were sounds of prayer from a nearby mosque. The day started with the girls waking up at 5am to make breakfast. Every girl had a different responsibility for the week, which was written on the wall, and Usha ran her house strictly. The girls would either make breakfast, help the younger ones get up and brush their teeth, wash laundry or work on homework. That first morning, I went to watch the girls make breakfast chapatis. They made the dough from scratch, then rolled them out into the most perfect circles, before tossing them on top of the fire, allowing them to cook. They prepared enough for everyone in the house including the twelve girls, Usha, and Usha's husband. It was quite a sight to see. The girls were far more disciplined than I imagined. I walked the girls to school just as the Indian sun was rising above the horizon. We held hands and walked in a double file line to get there, dropping each set of girls at their different schools. Some of the girls went to primary school and the others to a secondary school. At this time of day, the streets were filled with oxen pulling along the specialties of vegetables, milk or other goods that were to be sold that day. There was no sidewalk, just the side of the road and a hope I wouldn't have my foot run over by a cart. We dropped off the girls at school and went home. I took my first shower in India … and it was a fun experience, filling the bucket with water and then pouring it on myself as I bathed. Of course, I'd been used to having hot water at all times of the day, but there it was only during the daytime due to the solar heated water system. Anjali taught me to 'squeegee' the remaining water on the ground into the drain underneath the sink at the end of my bath.

When I first arrived at the orphanage, I had no idea how I could help all the girls. They seemed so disciplined, well-behaved, educated and clear on what their goals were. Then on the day before my birthday, as we were headed to the local market for a treat of chili fries, Manisha,

AUTHENTICITY & ACTION

whose hand I was holding, began to tell me her story. She was then about twelve years old, and she told me about how her father died a few years ago, leaving her with her father's wife. Her father's wife then forced her and her little sister into slave labour. Manisha ran away and lived on the streets for over a year, going door to door for work and help. Sneha was only four-years-old when she was rescued. The little girl had endured severe homelessness when the orphanage found her in the gutter. She was dirty, bleeding and had broken bones. Meeting Sneha who was now six-years-old, she was still rough around the edges. She would test me and see if she could convince me to buy sweets for her. When they prepped meals, I often found her sneaking a few peas into her mouth, as if she were concerned about when the next meal would come. Story after story was the same; girls who had experienced severe homelessness, abuse and challenges at such a young age. It was something I could never imagine enduring. Hearing their stories, I finally understood why I was there; I was a big sister to love them, mentor them, believe in them and support them through this new life with education. They all valued their education as an opportunity to create a meaningful life. They studied all day, hoping that this new life would allow them to become contributing members of society. Seeing firsthand how education was an equaliser that leveled out the playing field all over the world, it was clear to me that this was not only a core value of mine but a purpose.

Back at the girls' home, we prepared for the festivities of the following day. It was not just my birthday, but this day also landed on the holiday of *Diwali*, the festival of light over darkness, good over evil. Fireworks and light splattered across the sky that evening as we laid out a rug on the roof. We laughed about the fireworks that landed on the roof - something that would never be allowed to happen if we were in California. The girls wanted to stay up until midnight to wait for my birthday and we ate Cadbury chocolates and Indian dry snacks. The girls fell asleep on the roof before midnight, but I sat there watching the fireworks streak across the sky as they slept. The next morning, I would be leaving for Nepal. I couldn't be more grateful for the experience I was having, how it opened my eyes to a different world and experience.

In the morning, the girls woke up way before me and raided the room. They were so excited it was my birthday, and they couldn't wait to celebrate. Each girl had a small locker at the home which they filled with their most valuable possessions. The items were minimal, but it was usually necklaces and jewelry that they had kept over time, or items that other volunteers had given to them. They came to my bed with Cadbury chocolates and laid out their most prized possessions, their jewellery that they did not have any extra of. 'We want you to have it for your birthday, Didi Wendy,' they said. I was so honoured and shocked. Here they were, offering me their most prized possessions, even though I had only known them for a short time. Something within me shifted that day on my 28th birthday. I couldn't understand how I was living in Los Angeles with the nicest material items, yet I still felt like I never had enough, while these girls who had nothing wanted to give me everything they had. I could also no longer understand how I carried so much anger and hurt from the loss of my mother, feeling like the world owed me something, yet these girls who had endured their own challenges, were so happy and grateful for their new chance in life. It was at that moment I realised happiness is a choice - living in lack or abundance is a choice. That was the best birthday anyone could ask for; the gift of light over darkness and good over evil. The way I saw the world shifted, and most importantly, the way I saw myself in the world had shifted.

As I flew on the plane into Nepal that day, my suitcase full of treasures from India, I felt a deep sense of sadness at leaving the girls. I wanted to stay with them; they had given me a gift beyond words.

AUTHENTICITY & ACTION

As the plane descended into Nepal, I felt an unfamiliar yet exhilarating energy course through me. The Himalayas stood tall, their peaks kissed by the clouds, as if whispering ancient secrets of resilience and wisdom. This was a place unknown to me, yet something told me it was exactly where I was meant to be.

I found myself deeply reflecting on my life's journey. My mother's passing had once left me feeling alone as a little girl, but in this moment, I felt her presence all around me, as if life had come full circle. Her passing had not just been a loss, it had become the catalyst that taught me to chase every dream, even if that meant learning to fly a plane or traveling to India. When my father saved the three turtles during her illness, he unknowingly taught me the essence of compassion, the same compassion that allowed me to mentor girls in India, not just for their growth but for my own healing. No matter the circumstances, we always have the power to choose leadership through compassion. And lastly, I realised that the real impact we leave behind is not in achieving milestone goals at work but in the difference we make in another's life - through our words, our actions and our belief in their potential.

For the first time, I saw my mother's legacy reflected in my own path, not in grief, but in purpose. If love had been taken from me, then I would create it in the world. That was the meaning of transforming tragedy into purpose.

As we were thirty minutes prior to landing in Nepal, I saw the beautiful Himalayan mountains that grazed the earth. The closer we got, the mountains turned from white snow to green mountainous regions with buildings that extended high up into the world. I saw the beautiful clouds that continued to caress the peaks and wondered what this wondrous land was that I was flying to. I was not ready for the adventures that awaited me. From India, I learned about the gift of education and the impact it would have on all lives, that compassion is the bridge between souls, and the impact we leave is the only legacy we leave behind.

I wondered what Nepal would teach me. Little did I know, this was only the beginning stage of Building Education.

WENDY SHEW

Wendy Shew was born and raised in San Francisco, California as a first generation with immigrant parents from China. At an early age, she experienced the tragedy of losing her mother at eight-years-old, which became her catalyst for 25 years in social impact work.

She experienced firsthand how education can become the equaliser in anyone's life.

She studied aviation, learned to fly single engine prop planes, and worked in the international aviation business as a jet engine specialist. After volunteering in October 2014 at a girl's orphanage in India, she quit her job 4 months later, sold all her things, and left the country to travel the world for six years, across Asia, Europe and Africa.

She spent a year in Thailand, teaching in a rural village and weeks in forest monasteries meditating with monks. Wendy traveled all through India as a solo female traveler, mentoring young girls. Her favorite experience in India was a visit to Vrindavan, where she volunteered at a widows' mission in Hindu temples, where currently over 6,000 widows in India reside. She coincidentally met the Dalai Lama and made her way to Tanzania, where she found herself worshiping with hundreds of children from a local hospital.

WENDY SHEW

When an earthquake hit Nepal on April 25, 2015, damaging 9,000 schools, Wendy traveled to Nepal three months later, to support in earthquake disaster relief. From there, she founded Building Education, a nonprofit organisation that serves to build safe schools in developing countries to end the cycle of extreme poverty.

Building Education's motto is 1,000 schools and 1,000,000 lives.

In collaboration with local governments, schools and partner organisations, Building Education aims to transform rural villages into prosperous, dignified communities.

Under Wendy's leadership, Building Education has achieved remarkable milestones:

- 5 schools completed, with the 6th and 7th schools under construction, serving over 1200 students
- 3 water systems installed, benefiting 300+ households with access to clean drinking water, reducing the death rate by 90% in the first village
- 6 villages impacted for 800+ households with 2 roads created
- 3 playgrounds built, fostering childhood development and community engagement.
- 3 villages with access to energy
- The implementation of hydroponic farming systems, growing over 320 plants to feed students daily and teach sustainable agricultural practices.
- A celebration of their first university graduate, a young woman now working as a pharmacist.

Beyond these numbers, Wendy's work extends to empowering local communities by partnering with governments, organisations and beneficiary families to ensure sustainable progress. Her innovative "Schools of

AUTHENTICITY & ACTION

Life" model integrates education, infrastructure and sustainable agriculture, creating a holistic approach to community transformation.

Wendy is also an ultramarathon runner and mountain trekker who has trekked mountains all over the world including the Himalayas, fashion enthusiast, model and title holder of The Global Citizen's Collective, Miss Nepal 2021.

A quote she lives by: *Well behaved women seldom make history* – Laurel Thatcher Ulrich

HARMONY BY DESIGN

YONA SIGNO

Harmony is not about perfection; it's about alignment. It's about living a life that resonates with your inner truth, where every decision, every relationship and every endeavour is in sync with your authentic self. So many of us are conditioned to pursue success in ways that feel forced, disconnected or draining. But what if the key to fulfilment is not about doing more but about doing what is *right for you*?

I was born in the Philippines and raised in Australia, a blend of cultures that has profoundly shaped who I am today. My Filipino roots instilled in me a deep sense of community, resilience and faith. From my Australian upbringing, I learned independence, proactiveness and a drive for innovation. This duality has allowed me to navigate different worlds, drawing strength from both. It has influenced how I approach business, motherhood and life, combining heart-led service with strategic efficiency.

I believed success came from structure, strategy and relentless action, until I discovered the missing piece; alignment. Through my journey of self-discovery, I have learned that living in harmony is a conscious choice that requires self-awareness, intentional action and a trust in one's own path. The more I honour my unique design, the more joy and success

AUTHENTICITY & ACTION

flow effortlessly into my life.

As a certified human design reader and a certified sacred space holder, I have guided individuals toward deeper self-awareness and alignment. These certifications have enriched my understanding of how we are uniquely designed to navigate life and how creating intentional spaces, both physically and energetically, can enhance our personal and professional growth. Authenticity isn't about following someone else's blueprint, it's about reclaiming your own.

My chapter invites you to explore how you, too, can live in alignment with your true self. Through the lens of human design, life experience and professional expertise, I will guide you toward embracing your individuality, optimising your world through structured systems, leveraging teamwork and creating a ripple effect that extends far beyond yourself. Imagine waking up every day knowing that your choices, both in business and in life, are fully aligned with your purpose. Imagine stepping into your power as a mother, a woman in business, a leader and a force for change, all while feeling deeply at peace with yourself.

It is time to step into your power and design a life of harmony that feels as natural as it is fulfilling. I'm excited for you to live authentically, ready to take inspired action. But the question is – are you prepared to go on this journey to bring harmony to your life by design? Yes?

THE POWER OF KNOWING YOURSELF

The first step toward authenticity is self-awareness, yet so many of us navigate life following a path that was never truly ours, shaped by societal expectations, family traditions or external validation. We push ourselves to fit into misaligned moulds, wondering why success feels exhausting rather than fulfilling.

But what if you could move through life with clarity, ease and confidence, simply by being yourself? This is where human design becomes a powerful tool. Human design combines astrology, the I Ching, Kabbalah, the chakra system and quantum physics. It offers a blueprint for understanding your unique energy, decision-making strategies, strengths and challenges, so you can stop forcing what doesn't work and start flowing with what does. It's not about changing who you are; it's about rediscovering the version of you that has always been there, waiting to be fully embraced.

I began my human design journey five years ago, first exploring my own design and then that of my children. What I discovered was life-changing. Instead of parenting from a place of expectation, I started parenting from a place of alignment. I learned how to ask my children the right questions, support their unique strengths and encourage them in ways that resonated with who they naturally are, not who I thought they should be.

This experience deepened my love for human design and ignited a desire to go further. As I aligned my life with my natural energy flow, I saw transformations, not just in my family, but in my business as well. Decision-making became clearer. Productivity no longer felt forced. I started optimising my business by refining systems, improving processes, leveraging teamwork and delegating effectively. By honouring my design, I found a way to balance multiple passions, nurture my family and grow my business … all without burnout.

If you are just beginning your human design journey, start small. Discover your type and authority, then observe how it plays out daily. Notice the moments when things feel effortless and when you feel resistance. Your energy holds the answers, you simply have to listen.

EMBRACING MY HUMAN DESIGN
Understanding my childrens' unique blueprint is one of the most rewarding aspects of my human design journey. It has given me insights

AUTHENTICITY & ACTION

into their individuality, strengths and natural energy rhythms. I used to assume that what worked for one child would work for the other, but human design showed me otherwise.

I realised that one of my children has boundless energy and thrives when given plenty of physical activity. At the same time, the other is more sensitive to energy depletion and needs intentional rest. Before, I might have pushed them into routines that weren't suited to them, unknowingly adding to their frustration. Now, I encourage them in ways that honour their natural rhythms, ensuring they don't burn out or feel misunderstood.

More importantly, I discovered how to ask them questions that resonate with their unique design and help them connect with their inner authority. Instead of telling them what to do, I now guide them to listen to themselves. Whether they choose activities, engage with friends or manage emotions, I empower them to trust their instincts. This shift has strengthened our bond and given them the tools to navigate life with confidence and self-trust.

But my biggest revelation came when I turned inward.

For most of my life, I felt as if something was wrong with me. I could never commit to just one thing. I was passionate about so many different ideas, projects and opportunities. I would throw myself into something with excitement, only to feel my interest fade before it was fully completed. I questioned my ability to follow through, wondering if I lacked discipline or commitment. Society told me that success required a singular focus, but that never felt natural to me.

Then, I discovered my human design.

Learning that I'm a manifesting generator changed everything. My tendency to explore multiple passions wasn't a weakness – it was my gift. I finally understood why I thrived when I allowed myself to pivot, shift and follow what excited me. Instead of seeing myself as inconsistent, I embraced the power of my multidimensional nature.

I also learned how I was designed to make decisions. As a manifesting generator with sacral authority, I discovered I'm meant to respond, rather than chase things out of pressure. My gut instinct guides me toward what is meant for me. When I honour this process, decisions become clearer, stress fades and opportunities naturally align.

Understanding my design has helped me create a life and business that work with my energy – not against it. It has given me the clarity to let go of what drains me and fully embrace what lights me up.

EMBRACING SPEED, ADAPTABILITY AND INNOVATION

As a manifesting generator with a 3/5 profile in human design, my life has been shaped by my ability to pivot quickly, master multiple disciplines and embrace a trial-and-error approach to growth. Manifesting generators are known for their dynamic energy, adaptability and efficiency. We are designed to move fast, shift gears when something no longer serves us and innovate as we go. My 3/5 profile further reinforces this by making me a natural problem-solver who learns through experience and shares insights to help others navigate their path.

This understanding has allowed me to lean into my strengths rather than resist them. I no longer feel pressured to follow a linear path or force myself into long-term commitments that drain me. Instead, I honour my ability to dive into multiple projects, extract wisdom from different experiences and integrate those learnings into new ventures. Recognising this has also helped me optimise my decision-making, ensuring I invest my energy only in endeavours that light me up.

One of the defining traits of a manifesting generator is efficiency. We are not here to follow conventional methods, we are here to find shortcuts, streamline systems and create innovative solutions that challenge the norm. I now see that my unconventional approach isn't a flaw – it's

AUTHENTICITY & ACTION

my superpower.

OPTIMISING LIFE AND BUSINESS THROUGH SYSTEMS, TEAMWORK AND HUMAN DESIGN

My professional journey has been a significant part of my evolution. With a bachelor of computing degree and certifications in project management and service management, I developed a structured, analytical mindset that became invaluable in business optimisation and process improvement. My early career in the university sector taught me the discipline of managing complex IT service environments, troubleshooting challenges and developing efficient solutions. These experiences sharpened my ability to adapt, think critically and solve problems effectively, skills that became essential in my entrepreneurial journey.

When I stepped into entrepreneurship, I applied what I had learned to create businesses prioritising efficiency, scalability and heart-centred leadership. By streamlining operations, I helped businesses focus on their zone of genius, rather than getting lost in inefficiencies. A key factor in this optimisation has been understanding the human design of my team members.

But beyond optimising business, I've also learned to optimise life as a mother. Raising small children while running multiple businesses has shown me that structure and support are essential, not as a way to do more, but as a way to do things *with ease*. Motherhood is a constant dance between being present for my children and pursuing the work that fuels me. It has required me to release the pressure of *doing it all*, and instead embrace systems that allow flexibility, teamwork and intentionality.

Human design has transformed not just how I work, but how I parent. My children, like me, have unique energy dynamics that influence how they move through the world. My projector child, for instance, thrives in an environment where they feel recognised and invited into conversations. Unlike me, as a manifesting generator, they are not designed to be in constant motion. They need time to rest, observe and process before jumping into action. Understanding this has helped me shift my approach. Rather than pushing them to keep up, I now celebrate their ability to see things deeply, guide them with wisdom and contribute in their own meaningful way.

On the other hand, my generator child radiates a steady, consistent energy. They find deep satisfaction in engaging with things they love and their joy is infectious when they are immersed in something that genuinely excites them. I've learned that instead of directing their energy, I need to let them follow what lights them up. When they are in flow, their natural enthusiasm fuels not just themselves, but those around them, including me.

I used to feel the weight of trying to parent in a way that wasn't fully aligned with who my children are. But now, instead of imposing rigid expectations, I honour how they are naturally designed to thrive. And just as I've adapted my parenting, I've also built my businesses in a way that aligns with my strengths.

As a manifesting generator, I operate quickly and thrive when surrounded by individuals who complement my energy, enhance efficiency and understand my rhythm. Learning my team's human design has allowed me to build a work environment where everyone is positioned for success. Delegating tasks that align with their strengths, communicating in ways that resonate with them and fostering a culture of understanding, has created an empowered, high-performing team.

It's not just about me as a business owner or mother, it's about leading in a way that allows my team and my family to thrive, ensuring that none of us burn out. Instead, we operate from a place of alignment and strength. Through intentional living, structured optimisation and meaningful collaboration, we can cultivate a reality that not only supports our own wellbeing but also positively impacts those around us. The world needs individuals willing to embrace their authenticity and take inspired action toward meaningful change.

THE RIPPLE EFFECT OF LIVING WITH HARMONY

Our choices influence not just ourselves but also our families, businesses, communities … and the world around us. By choosing to live a life by design in harmony, we inspire others to do the same.

As a mother, I have seen how my alignment impacts my children. When I honour my energy, set healthy boundaries and create space for what truly matters, I show my children what it looks like to live with intention. They learn, not just through my words but through my actions, how I navigate challenges, embrace growth and prioritise joy. I lead by example, knowing the way I show up in my own life gives them permission to do the same. By optimising my life and business through human design, systems and collaboration, I not only create a sustainable and fulfilling path for myself, but also model the same possibilities for my family and my team.

This impact extends beyond the home. When we, as mothers, embrace alignment, we influence the next generation to trust themselves, live authentically and contribute meaningfully to the world. Our families thrive, our communities become more connected, and collectively, we cultivate a world where people lead with purpose rather than pressure. A harmonious life isn't just about personal fulfilment, it's about creating a legacy of empowerment, resilience and positive change.

But I am not perfect, and my life is far from flawless. I am a work in progress, always evolving, always learning. I recognise the areas of my life as a mother, leader and entrepreneur, where improvements can be made and I embrace them with an open mind and heart. I take inspiration from my why, the deep purpose that fuels me, to remain faithful to my journey, to live authentically and to take inspired action each and every day.

Harmony by design is about crafting a life that reflects your truth. It's about being intentional with your time, energy and impact. It is about recognising that you are not confined to a single role but are instead a beautiful tapestry of experiences, strengths and evolving aspirations.

As you continue your journey, remember you have the power to design a life that is fulfilling, meaningful and true to you. Whether through business, family or personal growth, embrace the path ahead with both heart and action, knowing your example can inspire and uplift those around you. When we live in alignment with our purpose, we don't just transform our own lives, we uplift those around us, creating a wave of positive change that extends far beyond what we can see.

The time to step into your truth is now. Your energy, your passions and your dreams are valid. Trust in them. Move forward with confidence, knowing that when you lead by example and honour your unique design, life unfolds with greater ease, fulfilment and impact.

The question remains – are you ready to go on this journey to bring harmony to your life by design?

Yes?

YES!

Affirmation: *I trust my design, take inspired action and create a life of harmony with ease and flow.*

YONA SIGNO

Yona Signo is a multi-passionate mum in business, business optimisation consultant, and Certified Human Design Reader on a mission to help heart-centered leaders and mothers in business bring harmony to their lives through systems, teamwork, and Human Design.

With a background in IT service management, business operations, and outsourcing strategy, Yona blends logic, efficiency, and intuition to create sustainable solutions. She is the founder of Kaya Services and Vision Outsourcing, a virtual assistant agency helping businesses streamline operations and scale with ease.

As a Manifesting Generator (3/5), she thrives on adaptability, innovation, and leading by example both in business and motherhood. A devoted wife, mother, and leader, Yona believes in the ripple effect of intentional living, where small shifts in self-awareness create lasting transformations in families, businesses, and communities worldwide. Guided by integrity, kindness, and strong faith, values instilled by her parents, she naturally attracts clients and team members who align with her mission. She loves to travel, explore and learn; and is passionate about demonstrating the collective strength of cultural diversity.

Globally recognised for her impact, Yona is an award-winning leader

YONA SIGNO

dedicated to excellence and empowerment. She won the Silver Award for Women in Professional Services at the 2024 Women Changing the World Awards and serves as a judge for the 2025 awards. She is also the 2021 AusMumpreneur Gold Award winner for Multicultural Business Excellence and was named one of LinkedIn's Top 100 Most Influential Filipino Women in 2021. A multi-bestselling author, Certified SacredSpace Holder, Reiki Practitioner, and Well-Being Boost Program Facilitator, she continues to deepen her commitment to holistic growth and transformation.

Through her work, Yona inspires others to trust their design, optimise their lives, professionally and personally, and take inspired action toward a fulfilling, sustainable future free from burnout.

~ I dedicate this chapter to my children, husband, parents, team, and support circle, whose unwavering love and support provide me with a safe space to be my authentic self, to pursue my passion with purpose, and evolve along my journey.

Connect with Yona:
Website: yonasigno.com
Instagram/Facebook: @yonasigno
LinkedIn: /yonasigno/

THIS BOOK CHANGES LIVES

Proceeds from the sale of this book go to providing marginalised women in business with scholarships to enable them to receive support, mentoring and education through The Women's Business School.

Aligning with the United Nations SDG goals for gender equality, The Women's Business School scholarships are awarded to women in remote and rural areas, First Nations women, migrant women, survivors of domestic violence, women with disability and chronic illness and those facing financial hardship.

We believe that investing in women is the most powerful way to change the world, and these scholarships provide opportunities for deserving women to participate in an incubator program for early stage startups and businesses and an accelerator program for high-potential entrepreneurs ready to scale their companies and expand globally.

You can read more about the work of The Women's Business School Scholarship Program and how they're changing the world here:

thewomensbusinessschool.com/scholarship

ABOUT PEACE & KATY AND SPEAKING OPPORTUNITIES

Peace and Katy are the dynamic duo behind AusMumpreneur, Australia's number-one community for mums in business; The Women's Business School, providing dedicated education for aspiring and established female founders; Women Changing the World Press, amplifying the voices of thought leaders, female founders and women changing the world; and Women Changing the World Investments, providing opportunities for capital for female founders.

Peace Mitchell is a TEDx speaker, international keynote speaker, retreat facilitator and workshop presenter.

If you want your audience to be captivated by a heart-centred, warm and engaging thought leader and speaker then look no further.

With experience delivering keynote presentations on connection, business success, magic and productivity, there's nothing Peace loves more than engaging with your delegates to make your event a huge success.

If you've got an online or in-person event coming up and want to create a magical, warm and engaging atmosphere, please get in touch.

peace@womensbusinesscollective.com
+61 431 615 107

ABOUT THE WOMEN'S BUSINESS SCHOOL

The Women's Business School is a business school designed exclusively for women. Providing opportunities for innovative female founders to scale their startup, connect with fellow founders and gain advice and guidance from successful entrepreneurs and experts. Through the award-winning incubator and accelerator programs, founders receive world-class entrepreneurial education from a team of high-level experts and entrepreneurs as well as mentoring, advice and access to successful female entrepreneurs across a range of industries. If you're ready to take your business to the next level apply today!

thewomensbusinessschool.com

ABOUT AUSMUMPRENEUR

Australia's number-one community for mumpreneurs. The AusMumpreneur Awards are a national event recognising and celebrating Australia's best and brightest mums in business. Held annually, these awards recognise the incredible women who are balancing business and motherhood and creating innovative, high-quality and remarkable brands across a range of industries.

ausmumpreneur.com

ABOUT WOMEN CHANGING THE WORLD PRESS

Women Changing the World Press publishes thought leaders, female founders and women who are committed to making the world a better place through their words and actions. We believe that investing in women is the most powerful way to change the world and we are passionate about amplifying women's voices, stories and ideas and providing more opportunities for women to share their message with the world. If you have a story that the world needs to hear get in touch today.

wcwpress.com

ABOUT WOMEN CHANGING THE WORLD AWARDS

The Women Changing the World Awards recognises, acknowledges and celebrates the trailblazers, changemakers and visionary action-takers. Providing a platform to amplify the achievements, accomplishments and work that women around the world are doing to make a difference in big and small ways. We believe that by elevating women, their ideas and their impact we can create a ripple effect that not only celebrates these women and the incredible work that they do but also inspires others to take action and make the world a better place in their own way too.

wcwawards.com

www.ingramcontent.com/pod-product-compliance
Lightning Source LLC
Chambersburg PA
CBHW071956070526
44583CB00015B/1220